HEART OF THE TIGER

THE FORMULA

Rene Gillet't

TIGER PRESS

LONDON, UK

ACKNOWLEDGMENTS

There is nothing more powerful than the knowledge that comes with the heart that you were given, in my case, one that is driven by passion. For it is this, you will always follow to conquer your wildest dreams and aspirations. I have travelled many destinations to fight many wars, all believed to be in the name of love and understanding, for it is, the heart that is at the centre of everything.

GIVING THANKS:

I would like to thank my Mother for always believing in me and reminding me that the world is limitless.

I would like to thank my Father for being an amazing dad and is the very reason I am driven.

I would like to thank my Brother for his encouragement and contributions.

My Children: A. S. Gillett and R. S. Gillett

I would like to give a massive thank you to an amazing woman, Miss Dionne Reid. Thank you for the time you have taken out your busy life to read all my emails and being there with your words of wisdom, spoken from the heart when I wanted to give up.

I would like to give a special thank you to all the Venn Family. Nicolas Venn was loved by many; his passion for music was music to our soul and thank you Nicolas Venn for blessing our childhood with your presence. Gone but never forgotten xxx

The Team:

A Massive thank you to Helen Harewood (Proof Reader & Copy Editor) Jennifer Hewitt (Book Cover Designer) and Kingsley O 'Shea (Book Trailer producer) With out you amazing talented people it would have not been possible.

Giving thanks to everyone else: Thank you

"WELCOME TO A JOURNEY OF DISCOVERY"

"Externally I let people see.... what I want them to see ... Internally I am a map of different caves that lead to a number of internal treasures. Only those who are truly spirited will gain the knowledge and overcome the challenges that lie between them and my internal world. Those who succeed will be blessed with "the Formula" and the knowledge of all the rare ingredients that defines me" She said.

"She" could be any woman who is striving to find a place in a world that is obsessed with Definition.

THE TIGER PERSONALITY

The adventurous and courageous Tiger is a born leader. You are not afraid to blaze new trails, and, given your independent streak, you're more than willing to go it alone if necessary. Your firm determination also makes you a fierce competitor.

Your passion also gives you the potential to be a star performer; Colourful, dynamic and possessed with a commanding presence before any group. Yes, we can count on you to command our attention and generate excitement.

Interestingly, you have another side, like that of the playful kitten. It's characterized not only by youthful innocence and optimism, but also a playful sense of humour.

You enjoy telling jokes, which are made all the more funny because people usually see your serious side and are caught off guard to see you out of character.

This kinder and gentler side includes a genuine humanitarian streak. You are empathetic; sensing changes in the emotions and feelings of others, to which you respond with compassion and a sincere desire to help. In this way, you are openly affectionate towards family and friends, charitable towards everyone, along with being especially touched by those most in need.

The downside of the Tiger's overwhelming passion is that it can lead to emotional distress. When frustrated by certain people or events, you tend to become anxious and edgy. This uneasiness usually stems from the brooding fear about forming some contingency, leaving you tense and on edge.

Furthermore, your high energy levels, fuelled by passion, often make you impatient. You want to do things right away and can become deeply frustrated with unplanned delays. This rashness sometimes manifests itself as impulsive behaviour. In other words, this is the "fools rush in" mentality within, which means you don't always think things through before you act.

[And there it is right there, IMPULSIVE BEHAVIOR. It is the one truth amongst the over imaginative, uneducated evaluation of someone born in October]

INTRODUCTION

We as women often rely on other people's statements, whether it is star signs, books, tarot readings, our faith in god, friend's opinions and so on to explain what defines us. How the past defines us in our present and in many cases to predict what is going to define us in our future.

Endless searching and trying to piece together all the A's to the B's and B's to the C's like the spaghetti junction. It is after all this linking we hope to come up with the answers as to how we ended up here. In many cases still feeling undefined and then to spend a tremendous amount of time reflecting on the times when we were at our 'peak', a term which in this case, means you are at your peak when you are having the time of your life and you really don't give a shit, so the conservations with friends about peak - ness stated that this was the case.

'Peak- ness' is when you have raved from Friday–Sunday and you go to work on the Monday feeling like shit. However, you have this big arse smile on your face because, that weekend, you met someone and he's bugger booing your phone on the hour, every hour. You can happily admit that he will be good for days when you haven't got anything better going on and also how you can sweet him one day and blow him off another, laughing about it with your girlfriends because you didn't give a shit.

'Peak- ness' is when you wake up with your head wrapped around the toilet at a get together because you were trying to get yourself noticed. This is because you got yourself drunk, reminding people that you have no decorum or sense of where you are. However you are content with yourself (even after you were found unconscious, by three strangers who were staring at you from what seemed at the time to be the heavens above, because the bathroom light was so bright) and you were so drunk you didn't give a shit.

'Peak- ness' is when you've had the time to spend four hours in the bathroom creating pure perfection. Later, you realise that the person you did it for didn't even notice, but you didn't give a shit because you had the skills and confidence to put your efforts to some other good use…

'Peak ness' is when you can take a piece of PVC leather off a bus seat and then use it to put patches on your jeans. This is because you recognise that you are creative and when it comes to ninety pounds to purchase then real thing, the answer is NO! As long as it looks good you didn't give a shit.

'Peak-ness' is having three guys on the go at the same time; rotating them according to your emotional needs, and if one was not available, as long as you could rotate them you didn't give a shit

'Peak- ness', by definition, is when you are happy to do whatever, whenever and wherever, to whom ever and not give a shit.

It's funny how when we think of our 'peak- ness' it refers to a time when our behaviour was impulsive and many of us would happily give it another name to disregard the fact that we ever took part in such activities. I'm sure most women look back on their 'peak- ness' and smile, then again if your 'peak-nesses' were anything like hers, you would most definitely cringe at certain intervals.

"Only those who are truly spirited will gain the knowledge and overcome the challenges that lie between them and my internal world. Those who succeed will be blessed with "the Formula" and the knowledge of all the rare ingredients that defines me".

These are the words of a woman whose early life was very much about 'peak' experiences and the 'don't give a shit' attitude. She remembers having many energetic 'peak' experiences from the age of fourteen and they carried on throughout her late teens. However, looking back it was not actually the 'peak' experiences that drove her to her profound conclusion of self. It was the journey which she took after the 'peak' experience that led her to 'The Heart of The Tiger'.

Contents

Living a life on Mars 13

The Knowing 27

A Call from an Angel 35

The Benefit Trap 47

The Power of New Souls 53

Relationship with the Enemy 69

A New Era 75

The Definition Game 87

The Seed of Curiosity 95

Ingredient to the Soul 99

The Answers Always in the Question 105

The Search for the Definition of Self 111

Recognising the Warrior 117

The Land of Possibilities 127

Recognising Change 131

Going through the Changes 137

Recognising Your Peak - Ness 143

The Truth 147

Knowing When to Surrender 155

Would You ? 161

The Secret Ingredient 173

The Power of the Imagination 179

The Caves 187

The Internal Caves 197

The Internal Caves (the secret ingredient) 201

Making the Connection (Pathway of Alignment)   205

A True Definition (Her internal Caves)   209

The Ultimate Definition of Self (Her internal Caves) 225

A Taste of freedom   233

CHAPTER 1

Living a life on Mars

The 'peak' experience had led her to encounter many different types of friendships some lasted years, some quickly turned to enemy status, some served their purpose and ended with the 'don't give a shit' attitude.

All were born out of living in urban London, South East London to be exact. It has its fair share of cold concrete tower blocks and thick brick houses stacked together like dominos. It is an area that always seemed to be cursed with a constant grey smudge that made it possible to believe that either the cloud level had dropped or we were even living amongst the clouds.

It was a place where everybody knew everybody's business, which child belonged to who and where people were happy just to survive in the grey smudge, occasionally coming up for fresh air whenever they could, constantly looking for answers to how they had ended up there.

At the same time they adhered to the fact that this is life; A life with limited sunshine, limited dreams and limited aspirations. If the estate had a mission statement it would read "We are here until the clouds lift, God willing". Of course it had nothing to do with the choices they made, it had everything to do with the cards they were dealt, and this was typical estate mentality.

Even though there was no life on Mars there was a great sense of community. Children would play and embrace the diversity of cultures. Women would lead the household, creating small 'bitch cliques' to past the time whilst acting like clones of each other, with their fake brands ranging from Gucci to Armani, fake tans and their nail extensions (courtesy of the £10 a full set nail shop).

Local shops would stand next to each other, creating a long line of colour. Where walls that were once a blank space had been used to house tags of ownership by those who were lost, identical to that of the Berlin wall. Every night you would most definitely hear an argument through the walls, sure to keep you up all night. You could even repeat word for word the argument back to them if you was bored enough to do so. They all had the same thing in common and they all lived similar lives. Their brains worked in the same way as did their behaviour and they all experienced the same oppression. Yet the most amazing thing about this life on Mars is that you were never alone.

Urban London was at the heart of her 'peak' experiences because without the grey smudge and the populations acceptance of limited everything, friendships from childhood would probably have not have survived into adulthood. The 'peak' experiences would never have happened, nor would they have been shared and brought back to life through the conversations with those who were also part of the 'peak' experiences.

THE, UNKNOWINGLY, LAST 'PEAK' EXPERIENCE

It was 1995 and one previous 'peak' experience had led, unknowingly, to be the last of all 'peak' experiences. On the 23rd of September 1995 at 03.35 am aged nineteen, she gave birth to a baby girl weighing 6lb. 07 oz. The grey smudge that dominated urban London was suddenly present in the room.

Having fallen for a Dj during her unknowingly last 'peak' experience she was suddenly alone. Her only company were the thoughts of the past nine months; how those people with whom she had shared many 'peak' experiences with, were still having them (including him). She felt that there were so many more 'peak' experiences to have but somehow somewhere she must have chosen to give them up to bear a child for a man she had met a wedding.

The thought which plagued her most, gave her a very unflattering forehead whilst sitting in her bed that existed in ward 2B of the mother and baby ward. She did not remember choosing to give up her 'peak' experiences, it had just happened. She realised that these experiences had defined her along with urban London where she lived.

The company of thoughts she kept whilst being in hospital, took her on a visual journey through a photo album she kept in her head. She used the photo album to link her A's, B's and C's together as many times and as in many ways as she could in order to explain the present. Despite her efforts, she could not comprehend how she had ended up here. 'Here' she was in ward 2B; alone with only a transparent baby cot for company. It was as if someone had just shown her a mirror image of herself before she had got herself into this situation. She had seen many young girls living in the smudge, having babies at a young age, the youngest being only fifteen years old. Regardless of age, she had always thought that you could identify single mums because she believed single mums often walked around looking as if they had lost something. This something was the support of the baby father (child's father).

She often questioned the ABC's; the ABC's that her grandmother had taught her from a young age. It had been taught to teach her how piece things together when things did not make sense. For example, the grand question of "where do babies come from", when her mother was expecting her brother, left her grandmother to use the 'ABC' process to explain how babies were made. It was her grandmother who had always told her that the 'ABC' process would always help her to see things clearly. She had been working on her ABC's for years and wondered if it was a myth that sat amongst other myths, just like the tooth fairy and father Christmas, created only to make her feel better.

Failing to piece together her ABC's meant now having only her thoughts for company, thoughts that were overcrowding the section of her brain where she kept them. These thoughts seemed to be over populated with old thoughts and new thoughts; she claimed her thoughts felt as if they were stuck in a lift. A lift similar to the one in Charlie and the chocolate factory; ever-moving, zooming here and zooming there, one thought leading to another and then back again. However, the lift's last destination of the day was always the same, ending its journey at her last 'peak' experience.

Each time she delved back into these thoughts new things came to light, things she had not noticed before. These things could only be described as some form of bullshit. Now, she gave a shit.

She gave a shit that she was asked to have a termination of a baby that he had once asked for. She gave a shit that he would leave her for hours on end and not answer her calls. She gave a shit that when she was eight months pregnant she had not seen him for a whole eight months. She gave a shit that she had seen him walking hand in hand with some new chick that was twice as slim and twice a beautiful as she felt. She gave a shit he had not bothered to see how she was. She gave a shit that on the days he did see her in the street, struggling with five shopping bags (looking a lot like a pair of scales with a bump in the middle acting like a balancer) he would walk right past her as if she was invisible.

Yes she gave a shit! And giving a shit meant that the 'peak' experiences were truly over.

She and her thoughts stayed in hospital for the full four days, not because she dreaded going home with a new baby but for the nurse who came round every four hours with the big white pills. The white pills took her, for a few hours, to a place she was familiar with, a place where she used to go. It was a place where cocaine shifted her state of mind from giving a shit to having no feelings at all. Sometimes it was a calm, peaceful place where she could only hear her breathing and nothing else. It was a place where she could stop thinking and embrace the short peaceful episodes of some strange internal happiness, pausing to embrace the feeling of being totally free without any bad thoughts or painful emotions but more importantly having total acceptance of self.

Self acceptance had nothing to do with reality but it had everything to do with 'cocaine's' ability to deliver confidence. In many cases (during her 'peak' experience) too much confidence, where cocaine had led her to believe the unbelievable.

When the magic pills wore off, that un-flattering forehead reappeared. It had crossed her mind if she should get some of those white pills on prescription for the times when she knew she would need them. For the times she needed some form of respite from her company of thoughts, who were now becoming more persistent that she was beginning to give a shit. She was now anxious about giving a shit. She had been having the time of her life during her 'peak' experience, being 'off her face' and having fun is what she did and it was this kind of impulsive behaviour that didn't do anxious and as a result she had defined herself as someone who really did not give a shit.

The things that she believed had defined her were now absent. She felt as if she had been dumped, dumped from a moving waltzer which had thrown her off whilst it was still spinning, causing her to fall to the ground, holding that un-defined feeling, and now felt as if she had been stripped naked of everything she knew about herself and her world.

The 'peak' experiences had given her some basic life skills, of how to fulfil her own needs, her own desires and how to control her own emotional state. It had given her control of her own environment and after years of living in the experience she had given birth to her character couture profile which allowed her to project only what she wanted people to see.

Her profile resulted in her being known for being the loudest, funniest and egotistical person everyone knew. Stupidly she had used her real name and it did not take long for her name to become like a clothing brand; meaning she was well known in the smudge and not always for good reasons. Nevertheless, the bad had defined her more so than the good and being forced to leave behind her 'peak' experiences had left her feeling somewhat de- branded.

After two unsuccessful attempts to have those, what she called 'white pills' on prescription, she left the hospital and returned home. She had managed to obtain her own one bedroom flat during her pregnancy, the days when young mums were at the top of the helping hand list and when the government's agenda was to offer housing to vulnerable people. Gratefully, teenage pregnancy ticked all the boxes, it was not that the girls who got a helping hand were vulnerable; it was the increasing reality that young girls in the 90's were having their own peak experiences and often ended up pregnant.

She returned home to a cold flat and could not wait to turn on the light in order to inject some life back into it, what with the grey rooms and the cold mist staring back at her as she opened the front door, as if the smudge had taken up squatting. Days passed and her friends called and visited throughout the day, baring various gifts and cards, all reminding her it's a girl but there was no life on Mars. She was exhausted with the baby; waking up throughout the night on the hour every hour. When the baby did sleep, her company of thoughts began a game of question time. It was the game of 'Shall I call him', 'shall I not', 'shall I call him', 'shall I not' and when this became boring the game would change: 'If I call him, he won't answer', 'if he doesn't answer I'll give a shit' and 'if I give a shit that's a problem'.

Her reality was, that she had no idea how she should respond to giving a shit and it frustrated the hell out of her, to the point where aggression became her new best friend.

THE BREAKING OF BONDS

Eventually she issued her company of thoughts with an eviction notice after two months of wailing. It was like someone had just died. She had that broken feeling you get when you believe your heart is going to ache forever and ever and will never survive long enough to be given to someone else. During this time she had played flat line with the telephone, dialling his number then putting it down, dialling his number then putting it down. Dialling until the first sound which signalled it was about to connect, and then failing to find the courage to continue because the thought of rejection was too painful. It was painful which led her to smoke a tremendous amount of cannabis when the baby was asleep. Enough to send her into oblivion by accident and on two occasions she had called her brother and kept him on the line just in case she passed out. It was the only way to put her mind at ease, knowing that the person on the other end of the phone loved her enough to notice should the line go quiet.

When the buzz finally wore off almost three hours later and when she had returned from the place called oblivion she always promised herself she would never to touch the shit again. However, her impulsive behaviour meant she had failed to keep her promise every time. For this reason she had visited the place she called oblivion many times before.

It was not an easy decision to evict the company that had been around for so long, for they had become lovers. They had become lovers because she had often told people that she loved her own company so she could embrace her thoughts sometimes. However her company of thoughts were not coming up with the answers, if anything it just proved that she had too much time and her thoughts were becoming a constant reminder that the best thing about the 'peak' experience was that time did not exist.

Trying to steer away from the place called 'oblivion', she had found other ways to keep the company at bay. She called her friends every ten minutes, having long and drawn out conversations about nothing. During these conversations about nothing, she could tell when friends wanted to end the call but she would cling onto the conversation for dear life, to the point when the person on the other end of the phone told her she was breaking up and that they could no longer hear her. Then the line went dead. She would attempt to call back but all she got was 'hi you have reached the voicemail of........' Sometimes in desperation she would talk to the automated voice because it sounded as if it actually wanted to listen and she knew that she was doing it (hanging on to her friend's voices for dear life). She called this prevention, prevention from the company of thoughts visiting.

Her friends became great gap fillers and sometimes they would visit together and sometimes alone but either way she was grateful. She had a diverse selection of friends; some of whom she could talk to for hours, some she would not spit on even if they were on fire and some that were friends of friends. At that moment in time, it did not matter to her because they were friends all the same.

She had been defined by her friends as a 'social butterfly' and as the baby slept better throughout the night with age, she found herself staying up later. She liked the fact that her company of thoughts visited her less because it meant she thought of him less and she put this down to having great gap fillers who would visit and spend hours with her, catching a joke or two.

Her designated name of a 'social butterfly' was not reflective of that of a glittery colourful butterfly; it was more like a butterfly with fangs that spat acid at you just for fun. She did not mix her words and her friends often told her that she had some form of mouth decease. She was grateful to the mouth decease because it became a great asset of hers. It would have her friends in stitches but more importantly it was something that she had kept from her 'peak' experience. The mouth decease meant there were no boundaries in what she said; the words did not go through the cleansing process before flowing from her lips.

A fine example would have been the time when her friend Tasha ('Miss Hotness' to the universe and to all men) went to the toilet and returned shouting at the top of her voice in an attempt to embarrass her "Do you know you got shit down your toilet?" there was a burst of laughter in the room by the other girls that were visiting catching a joke or two, who were now waiting in anticipation for a response and they knew one was coming.

"How far was your head down my toilet?" she replied. The roars of laughter hit the roof. "No, it was just staring at me "Tasha responded. "It properly liked the look of your arse "she said looking Tasha straight in the eye. A moment of silence gave way for glaring eyeballs, followed by the heads which turned in a similar way to that of tennis match. What followed was a joyous outburst of laughter that shattered all four walls. This was the kind of friendship that developed after years of fighting their way through the group dynamics and one you would expect from four girls who had all grown up in the smudge.

Her circle of friends, like her, had no real sense of direction; she had grown up with them in the smudge and had something in common with each of them. Joanne, like her, had a fiery relationship with her mother and would often have that bad vibe about her which expressed that she was a hard done by girl who was going to fuck up anyone who messed with her. This had a lot to do with the fact that Joanne had watched her mum choose men over her for years. She had witnessed her mum being beaten up when the dinner was not on the table or when her mum refused to give him money to drink himself to death.

As an effect, this had given Joanne a permanent screw face. Even so, her face was blessed with thick dark eyebrows and she had a mole in the corner of her right eye that was often laughed about. It was defined as Joanne's emergency 'hash stash', should she ever need to pull it off and smoke it. Joanne's parents were both mixed raced; her mother was white with Scottish and Irish blood and her father had a mixture of Nigerian and South American roots. This meant that Joanne was darker than your average mixed race person. She most definitely did not have the appearance of the sexiest girl you ever saw. Perhaps it was because of the way she always dressed in tracksuits and trainers and wore a stupid woolly hat, a hat that sat on those thick eyebrows. She also listened to hard rap music.

Then there was Tasha ('Miss Hotness' to the Universe and to all men.) She was the kind of person who would freak out about the shit down someone's toilet. Despite this, all men wanted her (their girl-friends too). Tasha was confident, bold as brass and you would never see her without her perfect nails and her perfect weave. Of course, she would never admit it was weave, but you could clearly see the glue keeping her head together.

Tasha was the '£10 for a full set of nails' shops biggest fan and if one nail broke she was straight down the '£10 a full set' nail shop having it operated on. Her physique in the eyes of many young women was perfect. A perfect size eight that made her fake Gucci and Armani stunning to look at and she always wore high heels. No one ever questioned why. She was one of those girls that waved her arms about every time she spoke and guaranteed to flick her weave as if she were auditioning for a lead role in the TV programme Baywatch. Tasha denied that she had even grown up in the smudge because she lived at the end house where the grey smudge could scarcely reach. Tasha never gave a true picture of anything; due to the fear of being devastated by the truth for if the truth were to be known, it would surly kill her.

The youngest of them all was Tanya she was just sixteen years old, three years their junior. Tanya was the only white girl in the clique, however she had her patois down to perfection (patois being the native language of the Caribbean) and Tanya was very expressive when using it. For example, with words like 'INNIT', an alternative for it is 'YOU GET ME' her alternative for do you understand and 'SWEAR DOWN' someone else's version of the truth. Often all of which were words used out of context and deemed hilarious by the rest of the girls whenever she spoke.

They often took the piss out of Tanya always asking her why she wanted to be black and her response was always the same. She stated that she didn't think she was black nor did she want to be black, she had just grown up around a lot of black people and did not really know why she talked like she did. "I just do innit, it's who I am" "and "there's one thing my parents say they hate about me and dat's the way I chat" were among her answers, along with "I'm always telling dem that everyone chats like it ". This is what she would say and that's how Tanya got her nickname 'Miss Confused'.

She saw aspects of herself in each of these girls. Mostly because of the way they would behave in a certain way, in order to define who they were and even worse, they would do this to prove to the outside world that they were exactly what they said they were.

During the time after leaving hospital, her friends became her version of a baby father. She had given them the role indirectly and subconsciously manipulated them into carrying out all the duties that she believed great baby fathers would do, after all she had watched a few TV shows to give her a rough idea, 'The Cosby Show' being her favourite. It was her favourite because it took her away from her reality but more importantly she believed it channelled a positive message that not all black fathers ran away from their parental responsibilities and set the bar, should she want to learn what kind of man/ father figure she was meant to be looking for in the future.

She felt that her friends had a lot of potential, judging from what she had learnt from Mr Huxtable. Babysitting from time to time, changing nappies, helping with the feeding process and doing the dreaded 'round the block' walk. They were there just long enough for her brain to reengage with itself and were there for Christmas and birthdays. To her daughter they were aunties and she never questioned why she called them that, she just did. Subconsciously it had defined them all, so that her daughter would grow up and be smart enough to put them all in a box. In actual fact, she was unknowingly damaging her daughter by reinforcing the fact that everything had to be defined in order to have a place in this world.

CHAPTER 2

The Knowing

It had been twelve months since she had her last 'peak' experience and there were times when she found herself getting restless because whilst she was looking after a baby twenty-four/seven, her friends and him were still having theirs. Now she had that enhanced feeling at the age of twenty, of looking in all the wrong places for the answers as to who she was. One thing she did know, she was a mum. Her parents would remind her often enough:

"Well no one told you to get pregnant"; "you want to go where?", "Party? No more parting for you love" and "No more being young and care free. You have responsibilities now and it's not all about you anymore" were often among their comments. What did this mean? These comments made her feel like shit and question why it was only her who had to leave the 'peak' experience where she felt most confident and defined. What she would give just to taste the 'peak-ness' again.

Weeks passed and her gap fillers were so busy indulging in their 'peak' experiences she began to see them less and less. Her evenings became quieter and yet again she found herself feeling very much alone with that feeling of being undefined for company. She feared that the other company would come back and taunt her but it didn't. Instead, she was taunted about something else… the fact that she gave a shit.

She gave a shit what people were saying about her and it was all wrong. She gave a shit that her friends had no time and that she now didn't know who she was or where she was meant to be going. She gave a shit that her parents thought she was too stupid to be pregnant in the first place. She gave a shit that he was still having his 'peak' experience but more importantly she gave a shit about what kind of mother she was going to be. What taunted her even more was that if she was not able define who she was, how could she raise her little girl to confidently define herself.

For the next 12 months she tried reinventing herself and it started with her first hair relaxing kit. She had very dark shoulder length hair which was full of curls, thanks to her mother and father and their own interracial 'peak' experience. It was during this reinvention that her hair went through several colour changes from blonde to blue black, then from red to honey blonde. Her skin colour had gone through its fair share of colour changes too thanks to the wide range of fake tan bottles from Boots.

Endless searching in order to find the answers she needed, led her to the pathway of hundreds of books. She read the latest bulletins and she read about the latest fashions, the perfect body sizes, make up trends and so on. However, the more she searched the more confused she became and the more she read, the more she realised that she didn't fit any of the ideals. She had even gone to the tattoo shop during the re-invention of herself and had had her daughter's name tattooed on her right shoulder. To her it was a statement, a statement of love but she questioned whether, unconsciously, it had been a statement of definition.

It was during this time her thoughts were focused on her friend Tanya. She often laughed to herself because she began to believe that she was more like Tanya than she had originally thought. All this time they had made fun of Tanya, nicknaming her 'Miss Confused', she finally came to the realisation that it was actually all of them who were confused. They had been trying on different outfits in the hope that they would get that feeling, the feeling that told you that you had found the right one. In finding the right one you would, in turn, earn yourself a respectful place in the world. She believed that finding the right one would give her the gift that every young woman at her age wanted; self acceptance and but more importantly the acceptance of others.

As her mind set on Tanya it also set on the other girls. If you were ever to meet them, each of them would be able to convey clearly that they knew who they were and would always give detailed information to what defined them. She remembered talking to Joanne and asking her why she was angry all the time. Joanne had made it very clear that her childhood was shit, from her very first memory at the age of six, up until the age of ten. She had constantly watched her mum choose men over her (Joanne was not ashamed to admit that her mum had been with many men). One time her mum had actually locked her in the back room and told her to be quiet because the new guy she was seeing did not know that Joanne existed. Joanne had said that the whole time she had been in that back room, she had fantasised that her real dad was going to come through the window she had sat at and save her because she had that feeling of wanting to be saved.

Joanne had never known her real dad and knew absolutely nothing about him other than he had Nigerian roots, her mother had not mentioned that he was also half South American. It was when Joanne was ten that Joanne's mum met Dan and Joanne remembered that only four weeks after her mum had met Dan, she began to witness her mum getting beaten up. Joanne claimed that Dan thought beating her mother was 'fun' and he would often say this, smiling from his teeth and all the while glaring at Joanne with his eyes. He had her mum wrapped around his fist, metaphorically and literally. Joanne told her mum that she was scared and pleaded with her to leave Dan, but her mother's response was one of a cold nature. She insisted that Joanne was simply jealous.

She knew how much that particular life experience had shaped Joanne's personality and this was surely the reason why Joanne wore masculine clothes. It was not rocket science. Joanne saw men as powerful beings and had attempted to shape herself in this way to protect herself from becoming a victim and all her anger stemmed from the cards she had been dealt from a young age. Joanne had always lacked a loving male figure in her life. Then she stopped for a moment and laughed to herself, or maybe Joanne had worn masculine clothes because she was actually an undercover lesbian, she questioned.

Tasha on the other hand, was most definitely someone you wouldn't have your man around for too long. She felt as if she knew very little about Tasha. She knew that she lived in the smudge and both her parents had jobs. She knew that Tasha had an older sister who was born with both female and male genitals. The child had been identified at birth as a hermaphrodite but Tasha's parents had chosen to raise her as a girl and after a major operation it was official. She knew that Tasha's parents had good jobs and nice cars; however they lived in the smudge like everybody else. She also knew that Tasha selected carefully the things she wanted people to see and she never knew why, but she had always thought that Tasha's skin didn't quite fit. Even so, she wouldn't mind looking like Tasha because looking like Tasha meant you had everything that came with Tasha; her boldness, confidence and the happiness which radiated from her whilst in the company of others.

Tanya was easy to define; she was a white girl that thought she was black. It was not rocket science, if you were black in the 90's you were cool. The increase of black music and black artists like TLC, Brandy and Notorious proved this. Notorious B.I. G for example, was black music at its peak. The Fresh Prince of Bel Air was the highlight of daytime Television, booming in the USA with British TV companies following suit. It introduced Black sitcoms to the UK TV scene, like those of No Problem and Desmond's. These TV programs conveyed that being black was fashionable. This then brought some kind of unity amongst communities and began to bridge the gap between black and white. It came to a point when white girls wanted 'brown babies'.

Even though Tanya stated she was not black nor did she want to be, her behaviour said otherwise. Perhaps it was the way she admired black people and their characteristics, after all she had been around black people for the majority of her life. It was clear she wanted to try it on, just to see how well it fit. However, you still had your racists in the 90's and Tanya's parents were openly so.

Scanning through the lives of her friends she felt sad because she suddenly realised that those who had played such a significant role in her life for such a long time, were now questionable. She knew that the silence after her last 'peak' experience had taken her on many journeys in her head, but this was a different journey. This journey was about her and her coming to terms with finding what she needed in order to feel defined. She could no longer cope with the feelings that came with having no sense of who she was.

The friends, she had described as 'great gap fillers' called her regularly. Whilst girlie times with them happened a lot less, she still considered them to be close friends and was grateful for the times that they were there for her. Friendship was very important to her although, she recognised that sometimes it could be a hindrance as she often had the tendency to soak up their emotional dramas.

She regarded her friends as her extended family, on many occasions she questioned whether she liked having girls as friends because all they did was bitch and moan. They bitched and moaned about anything and everything they could think of. Men, Money, College, Body Size and Family, the most common bitch was about other Bitches. It was through these 'bitch sessions', she realised that she was great at giving advice and was able to listen to their daily drama's over the phone, listening attentively…most of the time, until the conversation went on and on then she would put the phone on the side, switch it to loud speaker, smoke a cigarette, make a cup of coffee, check on the baby, run a bath whilst the person at the other end would be still talking. Occasionally she would hear "Are you there?" and a simple answer of "yeah" seemed to suffice.

Tasha was the worst girl to talk to. She would talk about anything from last night's soap dramas, to getting on the train, to tripping over the Hoover, all the while complaining about how hard she had to work and how to get the guy she wanted to leave his girlfriend. If he was the type of guy who wanted his cake and eat it, Tasha was there with a pen ready to sign her name onto a threesome contract with its list of can do and can't do's.

This was her life, a life on Mars which was typical of smudge life. Even if she had been working in a dead end job, (of course not having any qualifications) and had no children, it is evident that her friends would still call and suck the life out of her with their dramas and she would still be holding that undefined feeling and endlessly searching for that something to fit.

He had not called for nearly two years. She knew what he was doing (the gap fillers were full of information and could not wait to be the bearers of bad news). The last she had heard was that his 'peak' experiences were truly over and he had finally settled down with some girl and she was expecting his child. "He's lucky." she thought. What she would have given to be at her peak for an extra two years. Instead she had spent the past two years struggling and knowing the challenges of single motherhood, whilst living a life on Mars.

CHAPTER 3

A Call from an Angel

With the feeling of living a life on Mars and all the things that came with it, became an institution. Her psychological state of mind became a place of care for those who were destitute, disabled or mentally ill. She had cried many nights but this night in particular she pleaded for someone to help her, whilst taking a knife to her wrists, threatening to cut deep into her skin unless god came right now, to explain why. Why had he taken him from her? Why had she ended up here? Why did she hate herself? Why did she give a shit? Most importantly, why had she been stripped of everything she knew about herself? "What do you want from me?" she wailed, sliding down the kitchen wall and ending up in a heap on the floor looking lifeless and deranged. Her eyes puffy and sunken were exposing the template of her skull.

During this episode of complete derangement the phone rang. She answered but did not say anything. "Hello?" the voice said. Moments later she whispered quietly "help me".

This was going to be the one conversation that she would have with her brother that would save her life and more importantly discharge her from her institution. It was not what they had discussed, it was what he said that stayed with her; "YOU WILL FIND WHAT DRIVES YOU". She had no idea what he was talking about, but those words went round and round in her head for days after. She wanted to feel them, touch them, hold them and talk to them but, more importantly, she wanted to understand them. Those words became so powerful, she started to use them as an affirmation and by doing so she felt them. At one point she even searched for a definition, with the hope that she would be able to enhance the feeling, but a definition was not found. However there was a reason as to why she did not ask him what he had meant and that reason was shame. It was the shame of not being as intelligent as he was, not being as defined as he was and the shame of having to show him something she had always kept hidden. (Her feelings)

Dealing with Defeat

There was a knock at the door four days after the incident. She thought that it was her dad, returning to the house having forgotten something for her daughter as he had taken her out for the day, gracing her with a few hours to herself. It was Tanya and she was carrying a long box which looked like one of those old time Ghetto blasters that break dancers stick on their lino. She remembered seeing one in the film 'Break Dance' and it looked a lot like it, except this one was yellow with bars on it. "What is that?" she asked Tanya, laughing. "This is a tanning machine", Tanya replied. "You sit at each end for ten minutes and you get a nice tan. I thought it would save you some money, so you did not have to buy all those bottles of fake tan", Tanya laughed.

The mouth disease could not resist. "Fake tan! Listen, you bought this because you think it's going to make you black in ten minutes, don't you Tanya?" she said, grinning. Tanya kissed her teeth and placed it on the table.

They both spent some time exploring it, seeing as it came without instructions. Tanya plugged it in and they sat at either end with their faces staring into what looked a lot like your grandmother's front room heater. "Ten minutes?" she asked, looking at Tanya with a concerned face. "Yeah", Tanya replied.

After staring into the furnace for a while, she closed her eyes and relaxed. She had visions of how she wanted to look after the process; she had visions of glowing brown skin that would brighten up her green eyes. She had never experienced a tanning machine before. She expected to feel the heat on her face but she could only see the orange of the machine shining on her closed eyelids. "Are you black yet Tanya?" she laughed. Tanya claimed that she was not even going to entertain that conversation and they both sat there in silence enjoying the warm glow on their faces.

When the sound of the machine timer clicked they both looked at each other hopefully, for amazing results. It was with a confused and pitiful look that she said "Tanya I hate to tell you this but you're not black". Tanya also confirmed that there was not much change in the way of her face either and they both felt a great sense of disappoint- ment. Although they knew that the machine was shit, they decided that they would carry on for another ten minute session anyway. The machine clicked for the last time and the tanning machine experience produced no results. She helped Tanya carry it to the skip where they dumped it, laughing whilst expressing how it had been a complete waste of time. Tanya openly admitted that her motivation for taking it in the first place was solely to see what she looked like with darker skin ".

Early that evening, Tanya left after calling the person she got the tanning machine from and had several unkindly words with them, mentioning that it had not done what it had said on the can, so to speak. Her daughter had been brought back from her day out with her Grand-father and as always she was given the run down of how they had spent their day. He told her how they had visited the zoo and then went on to feed the ducks and that her daughter had an amazing time. On top of this, she was told that she could make more of an effort to do things with her daughter and it was that sentence that led to a great sense of guilt. Guilt now ran through her body and she knew exactly where it had stemmed from. The feeling that she had now, she had experienced it many times before and every time she would disregard it.

The Travelling Definition

Even though she classed herself as being undefined, she had carried some definitions of herself from her childhood and into her later years. She knew exactly what they were and she had grown to admire some and hate others. Selfishness was the most predominant trait and she had heard it many times before. When she had previously been called selfish she didn't give a shit. It was her time and she was going to do things her way and as long as she believed in herself and comfortable with whom she was, she didn't give a shit.

Throughout her motherhood she had been selfish. Why would she behave any differently, she had always been like this. She had spent most her life doing what she had wanted and engaging in activities that would; meet her desires, fulfil her alter ego and leave her feeling defined. The definition of selfishness had been carried into her motherhood amongst other definitions and she knew this was why she very rarely did things with her daughter. Moreover, she had convinced herself that the things she did do, were enough and a lot more than what he did. (the Father) She knew that her own family had defined her as being selfish and she often added this terminology to a whole layer of other characteristics that she had collected.

She actually thrived off the negative attributes she had been given, it was a major confidence boost, a weird form of flattery and she liked being different. In her mind it made her stand out from the rest and standing out from the rest to her meant that you were clearly defined as a person. Many would refer to it as rebellion; however her definition was very different because she referred to it as survival.

The Speed Date

The guilt manifested during the night as she watched her child sleep. She stroked her child's head and had only the guilt for company. All the while she had internal conversations with herself. She battled with herself as her mind filled with thousands of thoughts, old and new, and amongst these was her relationship with her own mother. It was like speed dating; moving from table to table, move to one table ask a few questions and then moving on to the next one.

There were no handsome men at these tables, instead there were different parts of her brain waiting patiently for her to leave the previous table and join them. There, they were preparing to say the right things to woo her over, trying to be so unbelievably impressive and avoid being seen as pathological liars, hoping that she couldn't wait to get to know them better. This went on until she fell asleep, waking up the next morning and only remembering the table numbers. However, what was evident was that one speed dater, that she referred to as 'The

Shadow Self', had shown her what she had refused to see. Last night 'The Shadow Self' had her realise that she attracted selfish people and she was very much like the person she had worked so hard not to be, and that person was her mother.

'The Shadow-self' described how he is what sabotages our relationships, jobs and denies our spirit. He is what keeps us from realizing our destiny and dreams, but more importantly he is everything we don't want to be. He claimed to be the voice that tells us we are undefined, angry, and selfish and so on. If we do not own up to our faults and simply brush them under the carpet, in doing so he has power to run our lives. She also remembered him saying that what we do not like in ourselves we see in other people, and that we magnetise those very people right to us. It is only when we embrace our faults we can build a better relationship with our shadow and in doing so we will no longer see what we disown in ourselves in those around us. Even though she found him interesting she thought that he had stalker tendencies to say the least. Despite this, she knew he had given her food for thought and had shown her how aspects of herself reflected that of her own mother.

From a young age, she had known that her mother was selfish. She would leave her and her brother with their grandparents so she could swan around the world with her friends. It was selfish of the woman who had issues with her father to leave her children with him. A woman who had claimed that when she was younger, her father would try to get in the bathroom, causing her to lock the door and she had to put as many towels as she could up against the door so he couldn't see her through the cracks. This was a woman who claimed to feel uncomfortable having any form of physical contact with her father up until she was fifteen and lucky enough to leave home. A woman who's sixteen year old daughter had told her that the last time they had visited, he had called her into his bedroom and asked her to sit on his bed and give him a kiss, for her to realise that he was masturbating and still her mother insisted they visit, that was selfish.

The experience of meeting 'The Shadow Self' was evident, because for the first time she saw herself in her mother and it was their self-ishness that cloned them together. 'The Shadow-Self' had provided a mirror image of her past where he had been successful in showing her 'selfishness' and how it had followed her into her present. The word 'selfish' was frequently used to define her by many, therefore she could only listen and learn from 'The Shadow Self'.

From this experience she had learnt that she too had brushed her faults under the carpet for as long as she could. Denial had only led to her faults being projected in those around her like subliminal messages, telling her to look deeper and more importantly look deeper into herself.

Trying to grasp the 'Shadow's' logic, was like trying to re pro-gramme her brain into accepting and somehow embrace her selfish attribute. She knew who she did not want to be and she knew she did not want to have the same dysfunctional relationship with her own daughter as her own mother had had with her. This became her motivation for wanting a better relationship with her shadow. She now believed that having a better relationship with her shadow would mean that she could make positive changes and more importantly, question herself on a deeper level. She would have the power to re-write history with the possibility of being a better mother. However the experience questioned other things too.

Now, not only did she have the desire to be a better parent, better than the one she had been given, she also wanted a better life. It was evident now, that she was willing to embrace this speed dater known as 'The Shadow Self' because tomorrow she was going to start with selfish. She was not going to be selfish tomorrow. Tomorrow she was going to take her daughter to the park.

The Blessing of a Small 'Peak' Experience

After crawling out of her bed with the park at the forefront of her mind she knew that last night's experience had questioned everything. She even questioned if her past had defined her right up until her last 'peak' experience.

She had been given the opportunity to build a new kind of relationship, one with 'The Shadow Self'. With that thought, she walked into the bathroom and sat on the toilet. She described this as a thing all women should do every morning; releasing yesterday's soul. Releasing yesterday's soul (through the means of urinating) meant that your soul would not be riddled with yesterday's thoughts, people's opinions or all that crap that came with yesterday.

Whilst urinating and releasing yesterday's soul, her hand brushed her face as she wiped the sleep from her eyes, however to her surprise her face felt prickly. She quickly rose from the toilet and looked in the mirror. To her utmost horror, she saw that her face was red raw, swollen and wrinkled under her eyes. As she stared into the mirror in disbelief, there was a knock at the door. She turned away from the mirror and placed herself behind the door looking through the spy hole, the spy hole which had been placed there by the council as a safety measure. Standing there was a distorted version of someone she thought she knew. She used her scanning techniques, the ones she always used to look through the spy hole because without them she could never tell who was standing behind the door. That was until she became a master of analysing individual body movements of those she did know and she realised that the person looking somewhat blurred and out of shape was Tanya.

She opened the door and there stood Tanya with her head down wearing a baseball cap. As Tanya walked in she lifted her head and she saw that Tanya's face was covered in blisters, some joined like water balloons. Tanya came and sat down in the living room. "I think I need to go to the hospital and so do you by the looks of it" Tanya said. No one was laughing. They sat on the sofa and rolled a spliff. Tanya explained that she had already smoked three joints before leaving her house just so she could cope with people staring at her.

All ideas of going to the park with her daughter went out the window. She could not leave the house looking like this! She was afraid of being defined as ugly. The truth was she didn't want to look like Tanya. She got her dad to look after her daughter again. He gave her a lecture about how irresponsible and selfish she was. However, it had not occurred to her that her face could be like this forever, until her dad insinuated that there was a good possibility.

They turned up at the hospital; totally stoned and laughing like they didn't have a care in the world. Strangely, they were having the time of their lives and they sat in the waiting room laughing even though Tanya's blisters had started to weep from the constant facial movements. They knew it would be a four hour wait to see a doctor and that the buzz they were both having would last at least three hours, so they embraced the madness of a small 'peak' experience and spent the long wait observing the ciaos that was happening around them.

Finally after a three hour wait, their names were called and they were shown to a cubical where Tanya sat on the bed with her head down. Tanya was trying to hide the weeping blisters that were now getting bigger; however they were hanging off her face at this point. She, on the other hand, turned on the tap at the sink and stuck her face under it. "I know this is a fucked up situation Tanya, but we will look back one day and cry with laughter" she said. "You think?" Tanya replied. The inspiration behind her statement came from her 'peak' experiences where things had got crazy and in many cases, had gone badly wrong. Nevertheless, she always laughed about it after when reliving the experience with those who were a part of it.

Now with her face embracing the water that flowed from the tap, she knew she would laugh about it one day.

A male doctor appeared from behind the curtain and they mentally told themselves to fix their eyes upon him. After all, he was a doctor and he had earned a respectful place in the world. Still slightly stoned, Tanya explained about the tanning machine between waves of laughter, generated from sheer embarrassment. The doctor could not comprehend why this was funny because he had just confirmed that she had third degree burns and that Tanya had a very severe skin condition.

The doctor attempted to explain his next plan of action which involved bursting the blisters on Tanya's face with a pin to stop further infection. His words became innuendos which made the situation an even funnier one to be in. They laughed so much that Tanya developed a little pig snort and blamed it on the tanning machine, claiming that it had melted her nose. The behaviour they now projected was very much like the behaviour they had projected during their 'peak experiences'. They were having the time of their life, doing whatever, to whom ever and not give a shit.

They were given a cream that could only be acquired with the signature of someone who had earned a respectful place in the world and, with the next appointment date in their heads to check on their burns, they left the hospital, talking about the experience and how they were never going to forget it. This had been a small taste of peak-ness , the days when she used to laugh and not give a shit about what situation she found herself in. Those were the days when she had believed she was at her peak, never taking life seriously, having the time of her life, going with the flow and very much defined. Today was an adventure, a flash back, a memory and something that she could add to that photo album in her head.

The next few days saw her spending most of her time with her daughter, whilst giving her swollen face some well needed TLC and checking up on Tanya's progress through reliving the event from start to finish during long drawn out telephone conversations. The conversation included a lot of 'do-you-remember-when's', 'that-was-soooo-funny's' and 'never-again's'. These days were quiet ones, other than when Tanya called to relive that moment for the tenth time. It was during this time her mind drifted back to the park date. She knew that once her face had morphed back to its original state she would adhere to the commitment she had made with herself, to do more things with her daughter.

She no longer wanted to brush her guilt under the carpet. In her mind, being a good mother meant acknowledging your faults and finding ways to address them. She believed, regardless of her own issues regarding her childhood, that to be defined as a good mother was not to deny your child of a good one.

The park date came and went. It had created a warm hearted feeling, so much so that one day a week was allocated to do something creative with her daughter, because she believed that, that one change was the beginning of many others. 'The Shadow-Self' was very much present. She saw him in her friends and her family and she also saw him in people she didn't even know. Having met 'The Shadow-Self' on many occasions, he became a friend and using his logic, she was working on selfish. She believed that when she no longer saw selfish in others that would be a sign that she had embraced it.

CHAPTER 4

The Benefit Trap

The 'Shadow Self experience' had brought to light to what she did not want in her life, and that was to be a mirror image of her past. So she decided she would have to escape 'The benefit trap'.

She called it the benefit trap because everyone she knew was in it, their parents were in it and so were their grandparents. Being in the benefit system had the same stigma attached to it as living in the smudge. Those in the benefit trap were often perceived to have a grey mist surrounding their outer bodies, very much like a grey outline which had been drawn on the road to mark where someone had died. It was symbolic of someone whose soul had been taken.

The benefit trap imprisoned people in the same way a farmer imprisoned a herd. People with no expectations and no desire to believe in anything more than what the benefit system could offer them, giving birth to a philosophy which was passed down through generations. Those who lived by it believed it was better not to work, hence why many of those living in the smudge including children had a limited everything.

Throughout her life, she had been involved with the benefit trap because her mother had raised her in it for as long as she could remember. There were occasions where her mother had worked and this was when cash in hand jobs were highly sort after and easy to find. This had everything to do with employers wanting to dodge the taxman and employees supplementing their benefits. She never knew what work her mother did, other than the fact that she went to work at 7pm and didn't return until 5am. Her mother referred to these days as "good times" and "good times" brought with it not having to wait long periods of time for new school shoes and all the other basic necessities a child at the age of seven needs, to stop them from being bullied in the school playground. On the other hand it also brought the feeling of neglect and abandonment from 7pm till 5am every Monday, Thursday and Friday.

Her father had always worked, refusing to be defined as part of the herd and she saw him every weekend unless he had pissed off her mother. Then it would revert back to only when her mother said so. Both of her parents had different values and beliefs and it was a wonder how they had even got together and had an interracial experience in the first place.

Her mother was a feisty leader with an aggressive temper and if she had to control her household, and those in it for that matter, by losing her temper, she would. That had a lot to do with her grandfather feeling the need to be in control. He too had a bad temper and her mother had most definitely inherited those traits from him. Despite all of this, she always had all the best intentions and, with a little understanding, she was able to develop her version of love.

Her father was an extremely passive, black soldier and one of eight siblings. He was so passive that he spoke with very little emotion. He barely interacted in a conversation and would mostly listen. Even after listening there would be some kind of passive response. To women like her Mother and Grandmother, he was the ideal partner and the ideal son. His mother too was a feisty woman and also led her household with an iron fist. He had been raised by both parents, up until his father died when he was twenty-five, and was very much like his father in that he did as he was told.

His father often told him that 'for a quiet life, you must do what is necessary to keep the peace' and that 'a woman scorned is a dangerous woman' (He often followed that statement with 'never allow a woman to cook for you when she is vexed' (Angry). He told his son a lot of things and in his eyes, the best thing he could do was to teach his son how to be a real man. "To be defined as a man, you must bring in the money" is what he said and bringing in the money would mean giving up his dream of becoming a professional footballer.

Now back to her story. It's not that she didn't want to work; she just felt that having a child limited her and her abilities. She knew that she had no chance of becoming a professional dancer for the Notorious B.I .G, nor was she going to be the actress playing the lead part in the Cosby Show like she had always dreamt of being. She felt very much apart of the herd and she knew that her unknowingly last 'peak' experience had made her time in the benefit trap more permanent. She realised that the more time she spent building a relationship with 'The Shadow Self', the more she understood that she needed to escape the system.

Everyone she knew was on benefits and she had recently helped Tanya fill in her benefit forms and that was a gruelling form! Not in the sense that you had to offer a whole heap of information but the sense that you had to pass the test. If you didn't pass the test, you sure as hell would not receive any giro through the post every fortnight. That was the problem with being in the 'benefit trap', people only came alive when the giro came through the door and once the giro was spent, they would lose the will to live until the next giro came to inject the next lease of life into them.

She saw this as being the only 'Life on Mars' and she thought about how powerful that giro was in lifting the spirits of those around her. Even though she didn't receive a giro because income support worked differently, the income support still brought a similar feeling as the giro brought to most people. It was 'having the means to live' as she referred to it and it didn't make her feel 'alive' in the same way it made them feel. There was no Gucci or Armani for her, it just meant that she could feed her child and put money towards her gas and electric meter every two weeks.

Searching for the Way Out

Using the logic of her re-programmed mind, she explored all the possibilities of being a pole dancer, an air hostess, a holiday rep and even a night club promoter. What attracted her to these kinds of job roles was the opportunity to bring back 'peak-ness' but more importantly any one of those job roles could help to escape the benefit trap.

She wanted an easy job with outstanding benefits and this was typical of those who had grown up in the smudge. Outstanding benefits included flash cars, real designer clothes and all things that she could flash in front of the eyes of others to show she had earned her rightful place in this world. Her father was the one who had constantly told her since she had given birth, that her life was over and that everything she wanted to be, she could not. Her mother, being the feisty leader she was, claimed that her father had that view because he had failed in achieving his dreams. Because he had listened to the wise words of his father and it had left a bitter taste in his mouth.

She had always felt torn between her mother and father and she believed strongly that the reason she had spent most of her childhood and some of her teenage years being so confused, was because of the parents she had. She had a mother who had developed her own version of love, where her mother would say she loved her one minute and in the next she was getting out the belt to chase her around the house, threatening to give her some serious licks. Her father on the other hand was a very loving man and he had a very good understanding of what love looked like. He had never used aggression, but the messages that flowed from his lips were almost always negative. He did not believe in dreams and he was very much a believer that you are what you are; based solely on the cards you had been dealt.

For her, this had brought the feeling of never being able to grasp what was expected in life, questioning whether you're good enough, asking where the signs are to show you that you have reached your destination. Your destination being the place that you were led to believe was a place of total acceptance and internal happiness.

After some deliberation she realised that none of the job roles she had explored were suitable. She was too short to be a pole dancer, to arrogant to be an air hostess, to far from home to be a holiday rep and given she was never awake past 10pm she was to tired to be a night club promoter.

CHAPTER 5

The Power of New Souls

The sun was shining, there was a great vibe in the air and the excitement was overwhelming for this was the morning she had been waiting for. It was the morning she had spent a gruelling five hours filling in an application form for and sat in a musty university interview room for, with a panel of toffee nosed lecturers. What spurred her on was her friends and her past experiences because they had become the model of everything she did not want to be.

Three hours into filling in her application to join one of the most recognised universities in urban London, she had only written her name and address. The rest of the time had been spent writing the odd word and wiping the rubber dust off the application form. The questions that were jumping around on the page seemed to be giving her an informal Interview. She didn't have the answers, she didn't know why she wanted to work with disadvantaged young people and she didn't know what her qualities were.

After skimming over the application form, she believed that telling the truth could possibly hinder her chances of getting a place. This was a place defined as being one of London's top universities and she questioned if she wrote the truth, stating that she had grown up in the smudge, knew a lot of drug dealers, had an A level in bull-shitting and a B+ in smoking cannabis, would this make her more suitable? Assuming that all disadvantaged young people, grow up in some sort of smudge, knew a lot of drug dealers and came from broken homes but maybe, this would define her enough to earn her a place at one of London's top universities.

The application was the outcome of one of her speed dates with 'The Shadow-Self' and on that particular speed date he had introduced her to one of his associates, Desire. Desire claimed to be the best motivator and stated that he did not need permission to enter but the length of time he stayed around depended on her and her choice to resist or run after him. She knew she desired many things: good and bad, and this motivated her to spend the next few months getting to know Desire. She called her time with Desire the (ultimate) inner discovery crash course because with it came the ups and downs. Some desires brought happiness because they were small and achievable and the not so achievable and somewhat impossible ones brought unhappiness and depression.

The desire that drove her most was the desire not to be like either of her parents. However 'The Shadow Self' had already shown her that her personality had elements of both her mother and her father and whether she liked it or not, they existed within her. She was aggressive, controlling and selfish like her mother, but she had learnt to love deeply like her father. She had always thought it was a confusing contrast and always blamed having chalk and cheese for parents for her impulsive behaviour. Sadly, 'The Shadow Self' had also told her, that her desire of wanting to moving away from the smudge and become a superstar whilst living in LA next to LL Cool J was also amongst the impossible, completely sabotaging her dreams.

After months of embracing and continuing the inner discovery crash course with Desire, she was driven, to want to help young people who had experienced the same things that she had. She knew that she had no qualifications, but what she did have was life experience and it was her life experience that flowed out of the ink and danced on paper with the help of her hand. For the next two hours the ink danced all over the application form to (Usher's) confessions.

Recognising Verbal Diarrhoea

The first day was recognition day and she celebrated with a positive affirmation.

"Recognise me, for I am not defined. Recognise me, for the barriers I have lifted. Recognise me, for what I have written. Recognise me, for what I have seen and recognise me for where I have been. Recognise me".

Her expectations at being recognised for all she had done to get a place in urban London's top university had been lost in translation. Her father could not get his head around the course she had chosen and implied that she would not stick it out and that her impulsive behaviour would get her kicked out before long. Moreover, it was just another opportunity for her to prolong working in a real job and instead hang around the union bar getting totally hammered all day.

Her brother on the other hand was a little more supportive and whilst the simple 'well done' that flowed from his lips meant to feed her ego, it actually left her starving. Her friends on the other hand claimed that her going to university would be a good thing. Of course, to them it meant they would gain access to her student discount, which gave you 10% off at the '£10 for a full set' nail shop and a discount in practically every salon, cinema and leisure centre in urban London. Undoubtedly, this kind of shopping spree would start with "can I borrow your card?"

The Experience

Day 1

Today was recognition day and she had finally recognised the fact that she deserved a place in one of London's top universities. She walked into her first tutorial believing that this was the place that was going to define her. She sat down feeling lost whilst the other successful candidates fluttered around making the room look very busy. Whilst sitting there, she looked around the room feeling disconnected with most of them, praying that someone she could relate to would walk through the door. She started to feel as if she did not belong here and had looked in the wrong place yet again.

At that moment, the person who would be responsible for changing that thought, and the next two years of her life, walked through the door. As she watched her sit down, she had this instant feeling of sisterhood. Her name was Chance. She knew this because she had overheard her tell someone else her name. Chance had a great mass of hair that looked crinkled almost as if she had been connected to a pair of jump leads. Her hair was dark brown but gradually changed to blonde when it reached the ends and she had a size 8 figure to die for, the guys around her faces lit up as if she had illuminated them like a ray of sunshine. They could not see the streak of lightening which appeared from behind that cloud of hair, but she could. Chance had that kind of electrically charged arrogance about her that immediately created that feeling of sisterhood.

The clatter and noise around her calmed, as two of the university tutors walked in and hushed the room, insisting that everyone find a seat. This was her opportunity to sit at the same table as Chance but she didn't because she was too afraid of being defined as someone who was begging for friends.

The first session was introduced as an icebreaker and for some strange reason she actually thought it was going to be a session about breaking ice of some kind. Then she realised that what the tutors actually meant, was that they were all going to sit in a circle and offer verbal diarrhoea. She cringed at the thought and started to panic. What can she say? How can she say it? Does she mention that she lived in the smudge, smoke cannabis and hung around with people who belonged to the same herd and only wanted to be clones of one another? She shuddered inside. She didn't know anyone who had conquered the world, wrote a book, read the newspaper or watched mastermind or any of the other stuff that geeks did. She knew she was undefined, but a geek she was not. She was a product of her environment: the Ghetto (another word she often used to define where she lived).

She sat there grasping the application form in her head. What had she said? What was true and what was bullshit? Suddenly her heart stopped. 'Oh my god' she thought, when my mouth opens the shit is really going to hit the fan and I will probably be under surveillance until the end of the week, and that's when they'll tell me I'm bared. She then went on to picture her exit and how it would be a very public one, along with a dismissal letter that held detailed information of how she had made a mockery of the university.

Verbal diarrhoea flowed from the lips of the twenty three successful candidates in the room. One by one, they stated their name, where they came from and why they were there. She started to question whether this was actually necessary and what relevance did this have with working with disadvantaged young people. She began to get very irritated, when all of a sudden she caught a statement that was being delivered from across the room. "The increase of interracial relationships has resulted in these types of young people having no real sense of identity, hence why they are slightly more dysfunctional let's say. Just to add, I find them very different and it is even worse if the black parent is absent because, let's face it, most mixed raced children are fatherless. I have not worked with a young mixed raced person to date where the biological father has been present or has even been involved."

In that moment, something within her switched on like fire as she replayed the statement in her head as fast as the speed of light, fast enough so she had time to respond. "Sorry?" she shouted. Instantly one of the tutors intervened and stated that this was not a debate exercise and how that will come later in the course. She ignored this intervention and homed in on the person whose statement it was. It was a black man who spoke with a very posh voice, should you close your eyes you would have believed he was white and it was he who had delivered this statement from his black lips and, like a tiger, she wanted to pounce and claw away until she discovered the reasoning behind the statement, the statement which had enhanced all of her senses.

"I am mixed raced" were the words which flowed from her lips in the most aggressive way she could muster. "Are you saying that I have no identity and that I'm dysfunctional because I am mixed raced?" The whole room had an air about it and fell silent. She was already pissed off at having to listen to twenty three versions of verbal diarrhoea, having to bring her daughter out at 7 am in the cold to drop her off at the government crèche and then having to walk for ten minutes to the university, all before 9am. To top it all off, she had to sit in a room and spend the whole morning listening to verbal diarrhoea.

The interaction between her and her opponent was defused rather quickly, it was one dagger given to the tutor who insisted that she discuss this with them at lunch. Unfortunately for her and Chance, who were the last two to speak, they did not get the opportunity to do so, the sound of the pips went to indicate that it was lunch already.

She left the room claiming that she was not in the right place to be defined and that she had nothing in common with any of the other candidates. Who was she kidding? She missed the smudge and she knew the smudge missed her. She had totally forgotten that the tutor wanted to discuss the incident with her because all that was on her mind was getting the hell out of there.

She had the urge to call Joanne on the way to seeing her daughter at the government crèche and she quickly tapped Joanne's number into her phone. Joanne answered and she explained the whole drama over the phone. "And he was black" she confessed. Now she was the one sucking the life out of someone else with her dramas. She knew she had to at least finish the day, for not going back was like losing face.

Whilst visiting her daughter in the Government crèche, Desire paid her a random visit and reminded her that he did not need permission to enter, but how long he stayed around depended on her and her choice to resist or run after him. She simply told him to piss off because she had no desire to stay at university and she was having a bad day.

On returning to the university she wished she had invented an invisibility cloak. All she wanted now was just to sit down and get through the rest of the day. She wondered whether her father was a fortune teller, seeing as he had always foreseen her pathway before she even walked it. She was now adamant that she was not going to return the following day. She had tried it on and it did not fit and she would never try it on again even if she saw it on sale at T. K MAX. She would just have to find something else to define her.

That afternoon involved more exercises including a debate exercise; she did not even attempt to get involved because she was trying to keep the tiger in solitary confinement for at least the next three hours. Getting involved would be like preparing the meat for a very hungry tiger. She spent the next three hours planning her journey home in her head; she had missed her daughter but knew that they would have all day tomorrow because this government crèche was attached to the university. The pips went off and she gathered all her things to leave after spending three hours within her own head.

Ready to walk out the door and mentally projecting her middle finger in the air, she was approached by Chance. "See you tomorrow?" said Chance as she left.

The Threesome

That night she was on another speed date, but this time she was having a threesome involving 'The Shadow-Self', Desire and herself. Desire had informed her during their threesome that he was expecting someone and that he would very much like her to meet her. She thought that this was strange, what with both 'The Shadow-Self' and Desire being male. Now she questioned who the female was.

The threesome became a place for 'The Shadow-Self' to convey how he was very proud of himself and how today had proven that he knew his stuff (he had brought it to her attention whilst discussing her first day at university). He said that the reason she had disconnected herself from the people in her first tutorial was because she saw things in them that she did not like in herself which reminded her that she was still working on not being selfish. The conflict that had happened had been a direct result of 'The Shadow-Self' being present at the time. He was the voice that had told her that the sentence she had heard was about her (the fact that being mixed raced meant you had no identity and as a result dysfunctional).

However, he did say that someone else had been present during the incident and that it had been the work of two. It was at that moment she was introduced to Trigger. Trigger was a feisty female; her presence was fierce and she had an overpowering energy. She introduced herself as a vibration and during her introduction she explained that there were many variations to her and that all triggers were unique and diverse. Trigger explained that her own personal variation was activated by sight and sound but others had the power to trigger touch, smell and taste. Trigger stood there in awe of her own voice and stated that she had always been present but could only be properly introduced through the means of a speed date. At the end of her introduction, she finished with: "It was very nice to meet you. Oh, and by the way, that's a nice photo book you have".

It was after this encounter that 'The Shadow Self' told her he was saying goodbye as is job was done. He explained that their relationship with each other had been a blast and now that she knew that he existed, the way that she dealt with him in the future would be very different and as a result she no longer needed him. At last, his position would revert back to where it was before they met. Knowing that he was still around floating in her matrix didn't feel like a loss. If anything, she embraced the fact that she had met him and learned so much from his knowledge for now she had the ability to see the subliminal messages which constantly taught her something about herself.

Now she had to deal with Trigger. Trigger, on the other hand, could be a problem and the fact that she was a female meant that there was bound to be a power struggle at some point.

Day 2

She was woken up by Desire at 6.30am the following day and before she realised what she had committed to the day before, she was out the door with her daughter in hand, on her way to the government crèche and then on to university. Whist on the bus, feeling half asleep and telling her daughter how much fun government crèche was going to be, her mind set on last night's meet and greet with Trigger. Her first impression of Trigger was not a good one and she was suspicious of her because she did not remember showing her photo album to her. Because of this, she thought Trigger was sly and the way that sly people were dealt with in the Smudge was going to be the same way she was going to deal with Trigger and that was to simply keep her at a distance, but watch her like a hawk.

Having dropped her daughter off at the government crèche, she did the ten minute walk to the university as she had done the day before. Out the corner of her eye she saw a woman dragging what looked like a child no older than five by her neck. "Fucking come on you little bastard! If you make me late for work you're going to get it when I get home!" is what she heard. The child looked withdrawn and fragile like a defenceless baby animal being mistreated at the zoo and as she looked on she felt this overwhelming sense of sadness.

As the woman carried on demanding that her child hurry up, she had visions of herself running across the road, grabbing the woman by the neck and asking her how she liked it, all the while shouting abuse in her face to see what her response would be. Instead, she put her head down and continued her journey to university feeling rather powerless. Her thoughts whilst walking to university consisted of photographic images of what she had just seen. She questioned what kind of childhood that woman had had and whether that was all she knew about being a parent. Her mind then rolled back to the woman's mother, assuming this woman had a mother, and she watched her version of photographic images of that relationship too.

Now assuming that it was the parenting of the woman's mother that had set the seed of parenthood, she concluded that it was possible that the women's mother had also developed her own version of love, just as her mother had done. It was the seed of parenthood that many mothers use to raise their children. This thought had woken her up and she realised that recalling the logic of 'The Shadow Self' and truly understanding meant that for the first time, she understood what he was teaching her. It turned out that it was not as complex as she had always thought it was. In this case, it was simple. We do not have to become like our role models or do as they have done, we have the power to see the very things that we don't like in them, in ourselves, giving us the ability to question them and we have the free will to change those very things in ourselves. Clever, she grinned.

Having arrived in tutorial with the situation she had just encountered at the forefront of her mind, she could not help but think of all the possible bad outcomes for that little girl because of the parenting seed that had been planted before she was born. She began to visualise being in the soul of that little girl and walking in her shoes for a day. She shook her head and felt rather sick, sick that she had not intervened; letting the woman know that her behaviour had been seen and regardless of what parent seed the woman had been given, could she not see that a new one needed to be planted.

At that moment she became distracted by the influx of people walking into her tutorial. She noticed that some that were there yesterday were not today. They had probably felt the same as she did at that university; as if they did not fit. It was clear that they had gone elsewhere to find what it was they were looking for. But one of the people who came back was Chance, who came and sat next to her. "You came back then" Chance said. "I did, didn't I." she replied.

The fight against Clone-ism

The tutors entered the room as they had done the day before; they both had glaring eyes, both grasping their cups of coffee as they had done the day before, they very much looked like clones of one another. As she became aware of them she became totally convinced that they were the reason she had spent all her life being rebellious.

Being a clone to her was like conforming to a type of ritual, a type of ritual that she did not believe in and had spent a long time trying to convince those in it, to rebel against it. She knew that her first form of action against Clone-ism had started at secondary school. Rather than go to lessons, she was recruiting girls in the girl's toilets, over a cigarette. She had a very effective marketing strategy and it involved psychological manipulation; identifying the vulnerabilities of the individual and using their vulnerabilities to identify the tactic that would be best suited to achieve the desired outcome. However there were only ever two ways of getting someone on board to fight the fight against Clone-ism and that meant either being nice or not being nice.

It was the not being nice that evolved into a deep form of aggression, for she had learnt that when nice did not work, aggression guaranteed an outcome. Thanks to her childhood, (which is where she had observed a few tactics of control, the use of aggression had been known to manipulate the outcome to one that she desired) Hence why, as a child she was often defined as rude and aggressive by most people and that's why she was the kind of child you did not want your child to play with and the reason why she had recruited many to fight the flight against clone- ism.

The group were informed that today would be dedicated to some exercises which would address individual views and opinions that existed within the group dynamics. Chance turned to her and stated clearly that the group were not ready to hear her own views and opinions and when she asked Chance why, her response was: "Why would they?" Chance then went on to say that she was now in her twenties and had been misunderstood all her life. Chances statement made her curious and at the same time very excited. This should be good, she thought. She thrived off the assumption that there was going to be a drama, similar to the one she had had the day before. She smiled at Chance, not wanting to spoil the suspense by asking her what she had meant, or why Chance had spent all her life being misunderstood.

The tutor (clone no.1) announced that she was going to throw a statement into the group and they were going to explore it. The class looked on in anticipation as if they were in competition with one another; individually they were trying to prove that it was them that was listening the hardest. She thought they looked ridiculous. Automatically she classed them as another set of clones that would go to any lengths to be defined in some way, as if being recognised as listening meant that you was student material, she sniggered.

At that moment, the tutor explained that in this line of work they had chosen, they will often enough come across situations that they will find hard to deal with and that some exercises will enable them to develop the skills to deal with certain situations effectively and objectively. It was then that the statement was given to the group who all now looked like clones of one another.

The statement:

"I would guess that mine is fairly simple and common. I always imagine being the victim, hands tied together and above my head. It starts slowly, always with my blouse, then bra (my fantasy men always enjoy playing with my C cup breasts first), then skirt, then panties; being stripped to garter belt stockings and high heeled pumps. Having my ankles tied together and being ravished. Sometimes it is by one man, sometimes by two. To make it more devastating, they begin by ravishing my ass first. Other times being tied into the same position by a boyfriend who, unbeknownst to me, has invited one or two friends over to meet, and ravish, his girlfriend!"

The tutor explained to the group that is was a statement given by a female who was only Fifteen years old and who had willingly donated this information in a 'girl only' group session about sexual fantasies. The room was still. No one had anticipated such an exercise. The tutor then asked the group how they would work with a young person who had expressed these views in a group setting.

She found herself trying to walk in the soul of that young girl as she had done so earlier with the little girl she had seen that morning. She had no idea as to why she did this for she had never been raped, nor did she remember being physically harmed (other than a slap or a lashing when her mother felt that it was justified). She looked around the room and noticed one girl who looked stunned and as she watched, she saw redness appear around her eyes and then tears fell from her face. She recognised those tears. They were tears of someone who had been broken and when she looked deeper, she saw that somewhere along that girl's journey her soul had been taken.

The girl in the room had fought so hard to fight back the tears so she did not expose herself but it had become too much and she had to leave the room. Chance raged for five minutes, insisting that the tutors had been irresponsible, however the tutor's responses were simple; wake up to the line of work you have chosen. If not, then this is not the course for you. It was with that statement that they were asked to continue with the exercise. Each individual went round the room expressing how they would address the situation. There were many conflicts and people were getting heated. Most of them lost all forms of decorum. Secretly she wished they would all get up and start punching the hell out of each other. Now that would have been worth going into university for.

The exercises flowed throughout the day including a number of team building exercises and so on. The girl who had left the room did not return. No one knew what had caused her to respond in that way but it had left something in the room, everyone was questioning it.

The day ended as it had done the day before and Chance approached her and asked her what she thought of the course and whether it was as she expected it to be. "No, but it looks like the right course for you" she said to Chance. Chance looked surprised and asked her to explain why she thought that. She gave a few examples of how Chance had participated during the day and as she was talking Chance sat down. "Oh, that", Chance replied. It was then that Chance made a profound statement: "Do you know why I do that? I do that to prevent my mind from exploding". All of a sudden she began to explain her whole life story.

Chance told her that her mother was a heroin addict and from a young age she had helped her mother shoot up when her mother couldn't get the needle into her veins. As a result of her drug addiction, her mother spent most days gouging out and when she was alert, she was back out on the road selling her body for drugs. Chance went on to explain how she had to look after her two young siblings whilst going around the house, retrieving needles so the youngest wouldn't pick them up and this had been her life since she was Eight. She did this because she feared that if she didn't take control of the situation or do the things her mother had told her to do, they would all be taken away by social services. She did it all because she loved her mum and did not want to be separated from her, even though it meant she had been denied of a childhood and on many occasions had to rummage through rubbish bins to find food to feed herself and her younger siblings. Chance ended the conversation by stating she was on the course to put all that negative experience into something good and the reason she gets so involved in things externally has a lot to do with her fear of having a silent moment. A silence that could be potentially dangerous in sending her into a place of darkness where she knows she would crash and burn.

She arrived home and could think of nothing but the things she had seen and heard that day. The little girl being dragged by the neck, the photographic images of the parenting seed, the girl who had left the room and now Chance's life story. Chance had told her, before they left the building that her name was not really Chance, but Sabrina Robins and she had renamed herself because she no longer wanted to be defined as the daughter of a heroin addict. She had chosen the name Chance because she wanted another chance at life.

Another chance at life was the wish of a girl who was on a journey to find the definition of self, one different to the definition she had been given. More importantly, Chance's profound declaration about another chance at life is what motivated her to stay at university for the whole two years; learning, evolving and graduating at the age of twenty five with a degree that would show that she had earned a respectful place in this world. Even more importantly, she had found a true friend in Sabrina Robins.

CHAPTER 6

Relationship with the Enemy

During her time at university, 'Trigger' had made many appearances but she had refused to acknowledge her presence. As a result, she had become aggressive, smoked more cannabis and she became depressed. Trigger became harder to control and the more she dismissed her existence, the more she found herself around people and situations which triggered her impulsive behaviour. Consequently, her university work began to suffer, as did her ability to be a mother.

The feeling of being undefined was at its peak and she had been called into the tutor's office more than three times whilst only in her 3rd semester. She blamed university for opening wounds she had kept hidden. She had gone there in an attempt to try and feel defined. Instead she felt as if the university experience had unlocked her mind to all images she had kept locked away, in the photo album she kept in her head.

Chance had been watching the whole time and insisted that she use the negative to creative a positive. She ignored this completely and was now leaving her daughter with different members of her family every weekend so she could party and take drugs , all the while hoping to re-live her 'peak' experience; the time where she was defined and happy to do whatever, wherever and with whom ever and not give a shit.

She had not seen Tanya, Joanne or Tasha that much since starting university. They were still having their 'peak' experiences and when she did call, sometimes they answered and sometimes they didn't. She relied on them to help re-create her 'peak' experience as they were all the 'peak' experience' originals. Chance did everything and anything she could to coax her out of this downward spiral, but for two months she continued to party.

After two months of partying and taking drugs, it was the dodgy ecstasy tablet which made her stop in her tracks. She had never taken one before but her failure to regain the same feeling she had during her 'peak' experience meant that she took one that was given to her by her friend. She felt an overwhelming sense of love and internal happiness. That was until she felt sick and the drug became uncontrollable. She wanted out because she did not like the experience. She became scared to the point where she became insecure and wanted to call someone to come and get her.

She had gone to the club with an old time friend who had sold drugs for years; so much so, his name too was famous in South East London and very much like a well known clothing brand. He was someone who was admired for the car he drove, the clothes that he wore but more importantly for his VIP status, which gave him the ability to get into every night club anywhere in urban London for free. Girls wanted him and were willing to argue and disrespect the sisterhood and themselves to get his attention. Little did people see he had obtained his fame and fortune from killing people and he had a bad temper and no respect for women. Hence, she could call no one. Instead she put herself in a cab and went home to work it out and working it out meant trying to figure out how she had ended up here.

The Awakening

She woke up in the middle of the night sweating and her whole body was numb. She frantically touched her body and recognised that there was no feeling and that the only thing that she could feel moving was her head, causing her to feel totally detached from herself and it was because of that she called Chance at 4am and said "help me".

Chance arrived at 4. 30 am and as she opened the front door, panic flowed from her lips. Chance could only understand that she had taken an ecstasy tablet and she didn't know what was happening to her. Chance hugged her tight and told her she was having a bad come down. After soothing and reassuring her that everything would be okay, Chance went downstairs to the twenty-four hour grocery store and brought eight cartons of pure orange juice. Conscious that her friend was having an insecure moment, she returned to the flat quietly and let herself in using the keys.

After being presented with eight cartons of orange juice, one had been snipped and poured into a large glass; she was taken to her bedroom by Chance, where she lay on the bed with her large button eyes and pupils black as coal. Chance explained the ins and outs of the ecstasy drug and insisted that she drink the pure orange juice because it contained vitamin C; the secret ingredient to make her feel better. On reflecting upon this moment, she was sure it had been the vitamin C that started a long conversation between the two of them which had involved how she had ended up there.

In the morning the birds sang and the sun rose, six hours after Chance's trip to the twenty-four hour grocery store. After eight cartoons of pure orange juice, she woke up and found Chance curled up on the bed beside her. With the sun now beaming through the window, Chance woke up to find her looking at her. Then came the tears of someone broken. Someone whose soul had been taken and it was at that point, whilst showing Chance her tears she knew that she had to build a relationship with Trigger, because Trigger was the only one who was going to save her from a life of aggression, depression, partying and drugs. However she did spend the next few days procrastinating and the more procrastinated, the angrier she became with herself. What was there to fear?

It had been twelve months since her and Trigger had met for the first time at the initial speed date introduction and they had both spent the last twelve months in a power struggle, one that you would expect from two women working towards the same goal. They went through the photo album together and when she found it hard to turn a page, Trigger would turn it for her. When she found she was fearful, Trigger told her she would find ways to become fearless and when she cried, Trigger told her she was healing. Trigger always made it clear that there was nothing she could do but learn to love her (Trigger) because out of all the relationships that existed within, Trigger was the one bad vibration that stayed around the longest.

Graduation day was a celebration not only for her academic achievements but for the journey she had walked, the challenges she had overcome and the choices she had made. She had chosen to share her knowledge of the relationships she had encountered with Chance and as a result, Chance no longer felt the need to be the centre of attention nor did she fight not to be defined as the daughter of a heroin addict. As for her the feeling of being undefined, it was still present but now she had found some form of internal happiness, with a potential career in working with vulnerable young people. She embraced her new title which increased her possibilities. Her university experience had now given her something she could show to people so that they could see that she had earned a respectful place in the world.

The Formula

CHAPTER 7

A New Era

It had been a while since she had seen Joanne, Tasha and Tanya and, courtesy of the benefit system, a weekend trip to Amsterdam had brought them all together. During her university experience she had never declared that she was in full time education so some of the money that she had saved paid for the tickets for all four of them to go on a weekend bonding session. The university experience had not changed her in the way that she had thought it would. She still knew the rules of the street, continued to use the language and still had an eye for an opportunity; especially when it came to stolen goods.

The arrangement was for all of them to meet up at her flat; the one on the third floor of a building that contained 250 flats and was based in the heart of the smudge. The building too had conformed to its own version of clone-ism, as each flat looked exactly the same as the one next to it. The only thing that slightly separated them was the colour that had been used to paint the front doors. It would not be the place that you would usually expect to find a university graduate living, with its dark stairwells and its numerous cans of tenants' and Special-brew lying on their backs looking rather abandoned.

It was a place where teenagers would linger with their hoodie's up, trying to look intimidating and show that this is who they were. As dark as their life was, they were proud of themselves but more importantly, projected that they were proud of being a part of a notorious gang. To them, this defined them. To her, they were just a group of teenagers who had conformed to a different type of clone-ism, they just didn't know it yet.

The Magic Land of Alice

Whilst she was waiting for at least one of them to turn up on time, she understood how the university experience had taught her that she hated being late and hated late people. Funny that, she thought, prior to university she was never on time. From a young age she had been busy living in 'The Magic land of Alice' to escape a life on Mars. She had spent most of her days daydreaming and creating fantasies in her head of how secret passages where going to lead her to the future. Everyday travelling down a secret passage, just so she could see it, with each passage having a different ending. That was until she had found the key to the passage that led to stardom at the age of fifteen. It had shown her that she was going to be a professional dancer for the Notorious B.I.G, which is why she had spent so much time practicing the running man in the mirror with a hair brush whilst listening to Mr Notorious B.I.G himself, often making her late for everything .

She had walked that passage and held onto that future in her hands until she was nineteen. It had been a long time since she had visited those secret passages and the last time she visited had been the day before she had found out she was pregnant. Lateness for everything else after that had everything to do with living a life on Mars.

The flight to Amsterdam was to leave London city airport at 13.45pm, yet Joanne, Tanya and Tasha had not arrived at her flat and it was approaching 12.30pm. Before she could pick up her phone, ready to let her tiger lose there was a knock at the door. Joanne and Tanya (Miss confused) stood there both looking very much like Kevin and Perry go large, except they were not off to Ibiza, they were going to Amsterdam.

Joanne stood there with the same aggressive attitude, wearing that same stupid woolly hat that sat on those heavy dark eyebrows. Her eyes were peering over the top of sunglasses that matched the black body warmer that she was wearing. But there was something new about Tanya, she was wearing a thick gold chain and attached to it was a cross full of white diamonds. She also noticed that Tanya had a tattoo on her neck of a simple letter C. They both entered the flat lugging three large suitcases behind them, and then Tasha (Miss Hotness of the Universe and to all men) appeared, tapping on the window. Tasha was already moaning that she had broken a nail and asked if they had a '£10 a full set' nail shop in Amsterdam as she walked through the door. "They don't have pounds in the Netherlands" Joanne said and there was a roar of laughter for none of them had thought that Joanne was that intelligent.

To her the girls projected everything she was and she admired everything about them, including how different they were from her. Previously she had thought that her friends were everything that she didn't want to be, but her time at university had shifted her thought process and ever since then she made a pact with herself that she would never disregarded them .If it had not been for them she would have never survived her darkest moments. If one day in the future that thought should change, then that would be a sign that she had lost herself. To her, having a degree made her no different from them. She had still been brought up in the smudge and experienced the same things. She was fully aware that her parents didn't like them but she too, was a person that a parent didn't like.

The Running Away From

After three hours of travelling they had landed in Schiphol airport. She was so excited and she knew that she had felt this feeling before; it was the feeling she had felt during her last peak experience. She was in Amsterdam and she didn't give a shit, this was a weekend to do whatever, wherever and with whom ever and not give a shit.

She was in a place where she was invisible; the overpowering need to be defined was invisible too. It had been apparent after she had graduated, that her family and the society in which she lived now expected her to do something that they could use to define her because in defining her they were defining themselves. A parent of… A sister of… A Brother of …. A cousin of… and in doing this they each would find a form of internal happiness for themselves. She didn't realise that obtaining a degree would give people the power to expect more and become more overpowering in demanding more, hence why before leaving for Amsterdam she had been bombarded with questions and statements; "when do you plan to get a job?", "I'm tired of people asking me what do you do and I have nothing to say to them?",

"Don't you want people to be proud of you and have something nice to say for a change?". However, there was one statement that triggered all her senses; "Do you plan to bring your daughter up in the benefit system for the rest of her life?" As these questions and statements bounced from all different directions they triggered a memory of what she did, the last time she felt under attack. It was with this thought she said fuck this, and brought three tickets to Amsterdam.

As they dragged their luggage over cobbled roads, admiring the canals and the cute bridges they walked over, she couldn't help but notice that everyone looked different. She was amazed how the people of Amsterdam were all individually different from the person they walked passed or the person they stood next to. They all projected a presence, one that gave the message of freedom, the freedom that she so craved, the freedom just to be herself with no strings attached. She had spent such a long time trying to pull off the labels that had been attached to her, she didn't even know how she had collected so many, but she knew that none of the statements attached to them belonged to her. How could they, she had never defined herself in the same way and now she did not know who she was, other than what she had learned from the statements that had flown from the mouths of those who claimed to know her.

The Map with No Sense

Whilst walking and following a map which Joanne had purchased before exiting Amsterdam central train station, they realised they were lost and to them every street looked the same. Little did they know that they had already passed the place that they were searching for twice because they were too busy being busy with each other. To busy comforting Tasha who was wining about how the cobbled streets where attacking her heels and why they were stopping every few seconds to wait for her. Now they were yet again standing outside the Grasshopper coffee shop, looking confused.

None of them had been to Amsterdam before and the map had become a trusted guide. They were sure it would lead them to where they were meant to be but for some reason the map did not make sense and as a result she decided to go to plan B and use what god had given her the day she was born and that was her mouth. She used it in the way of asking.

Her patience was wearing thin and unfortunately for them, asking for help had only added to the pressure that they were already experiencing. Each person she asked presented her with their knowledge of how to get there but, to her, that did not make sense in relation to the map. Even though she had lost confidence in the map she followed it anyway. They walked round and round, questioning this and question that. Questioning as to why the person had told them to go in that direction because it seemed to be taking them away from the hotel's location. By this time, all they wanted to do was get there and relax.

Trying to feel their way, they came across a man who looked in his early forties judging from the way he was dressed and the appearance of his grey roots. He was standing outside a sex shop; staring at all four of them and when her eyes met his he retreated back into the sex shop doorway as if to hide. To her, this enhanced his presence and she could feel him even though she could not see him. She felt as if they were walking into his moment.

She caught a glimpse of him rubbing his olive skin and as she and the girls drew nearer the feeling of walking into his moment became stronger. For some reason she sensed a predator and this caused her to become fearful. Why was she fearful when she had written her own book of predators in her head? It was a real life survival manual which had often saved her from the predators of the smudge and those present during her peak experiences. She began to panic and began flicking through the pages that belonged to her book of predators. The stay calm pages appear one after another and she became frustrated. They were not what she was looking for. What she was looking for, were the action pages. It was evident that it had been a long time since she had looked in that book; since it had been nearly four years since her last peak experience.

Her book of predators could not help and she and her girls had just walked into his moment. She took a deep breath as she saw him step out from the doorway. "Live sex show?" the man asked. She was still flicking through her book of predators, refusing to admit defeat, convincing herself the book was deliberately being defiant because she had previously ripped out some of the action pages. Her book of predators had failed her on three occasions and as a result she had ripped out the action pages that hadn't worked, even so, she was damn sure she was not going to become a victim again and continued flicking adamantly. She found one action page that she had named 'The One Second façade'. During his moment, she quickly changed her persona to one that she deemed more suitable, one that did not give off the "I'm a tourist" and she projected this one instead.

Joanne, Tanya and Tasha were totally oblivious to the process that had just happened in her head; she questioned how they could not notice him or her fear for that matter. Joanne decided to engage in a conversation with the man and started by asking why an old man was standing outside a sex shop in the first place. Joanne had an enchanting way about her that was admired by the others. It was aggressive but soft and she had a knack for taking the piss out of someone but make it sound as if she was paying them a compliment. It was this that made Joanne, Joanne. During the conversation between Joanne and the man, (who the girls were now defining as an OAP sex god) assuming that he must know every sex position that ever existed, she was frantically praying that Joanne would not give away the fact that they were tourists, for if they were to be exposed, this could change his perception of them, making them vulnerable.

Although the man engaged in a warm heart felt conversation with each of them and talked about all the places to visit, along with introducing them to his family and taking them on a visual tour of his home to meet his estranged wife, his three kids and a dog called Boner, she was not quite convinced that he was not a predator because she felt he had all the characteristics of one. She had not yet met or learnt to rely of her intuition. After promising to attend his live sex show the next day, he kindly helped them on their way to where they could have been ages ago.

Now doubting the Map which made absolutely no sense, they walked across the cobbled streets of Amsterdam; following the directions they had been given. All the while, she visited the busiest part of her brain that existed in her head and questioned how the map that they were following had led them to a particular place, at a particular time, where they had met a particular person "Was life like a map?" Is what she was asking.

Do we follow a similar kind of map that is meant to be taking us somewhere and, because of all the distractions and the busyness that happens along the way; is it this that gets us lost? When you ask where you are meant to be going, is it the interpretation of others that leads you on the pathway to nowhere, causing you to experience other things that you end up questioning too? Only to then ask if where you ended up was intentional and whether it was meant to be or was it all accidental? She laughed, because she was now questioning if she thought a bit too much.

The Morphing of Alice Land

The trip to Amsterdam had provoked another peak experience. No one gave a shit how many space cakes they ate, how many sex toys they played with or how many live sex shows they went to see. No one cared about how many steep stairwells they had to climb in order to reach to the place that was now defined as home. For her, Amsterdam was like a drug, a solution and an opportunity to escape everything and everyone.

At this moment in time, she did not want to think about how all her previous experiences had led her to where she was. She often questioned how she ended up there, her words in sync with those living in the smudge. She began to think about him and her daughter. She wondered whether he thought about her and his daughter even though he had another child. How giving a shit had caused her so much pain and that there was a good possibility that university was not enough to earn a respectful pace in the world.

Amsterdam became the place for citizen deliberation, except this type of citizen deliberation did not include respect. A deliberation, that took place in a small musty room where the girls were laughing at the conversation that had led to a passionate cussing session. This was often the outcome when someone's views and opinions touched the nerve of another.

A room full of hundreds of memories flowing from their lips, whilst their brains were working overtime to pick the brain cell they hoped would trigger an actual truth and when that failed they went on picking to find another, one that they hoped would trigger a true response. It never worked because these four young women had grown up in the smudge and in the smudge, everything was exaggerated.

She knew why every woman she knew did it (exaggerated the

truth)and she would internally admit that she would add things to make her story more exciting and admit to taking things away to prevent shame or disappointment. She knew there were some women who had somehow mastered this to perfection, so much so it blinded them from knowing, feeling and seeing the truth. And those that had worked so hard to master it had given birth to something that would protect and honour them until they were willing to wake up and that something was denial. Tasha (Miss Hotness to the Universe and to all men) was a prime example.

The citizen deliberation made her question many things. This included thinking how weird it was, that in Amsterdam they called a spliff a joint. That thought alone led to many other thoughts and whilst puffing on the end of a roach she suddenly blurted it out "I wonder who I would have been if I had grown up in Amsterdam?" She was back in 'The Magic Land of Alice' but this time she was taking her girls with her.

After engaging them in a brief introduction, she began leading them to the secret passage that led to four doors. The names of each of them were written in Lucinda handwriting. Behind each door there was a parallel universe and one by one they opened the door and stood there with their magic pen ready to walk in and re write themselves and their history. It was the most endearing thing they had ever done together and lying on separate beds holding a spliff in each of their hands, they each waited in anticipation to hear the stories that would fill the room of how each of them would use the magic pen to re-write themselves and their history in a parallel universe.

Joanne was the first to fill the room. She used the magic pen to erase every aspect of her childhood and she filled it with two loving parents, a suburban house in the heart of Los Angeles and a place at the Los Angeles Academy College of Music. As the picture clouds appeared over her head, her face lit up and she spoke with passion and as she told her story, she got so excited she jumped up from the bed and started beat boxing as to give a sample of the magic that would have been born out of the recording studio. "I would have been an outstanding music producer" she said, sitting back down on the edge of her bed.

Tasha (Miss Hotness to the Universe and to all men) had erased nothing about herself. Instead she erased her wardrobe and used her magic pen to design a new one. This one was bigger with six sliding mirror doors full of designer originals and as her words filled the room she went crazy, waving her arms, rolling around on the bed like she had stomach cramp and ranting about how great her pen was and if she had a pen like it, she would be drawing Christian Louboutin shoes all day every day. She had even given herself a pair of designer Sean Paul glasses, explaining how when she wore them, she had enhanced visibility and could see into the future. It was at this point Tanya interrupted and said "No that is God sending you a message telling you, you need to open your God damn eyes girl". Tasha raised her eyebrows and rocked her head from side to side as if her neck was going to give way, whilst the others laughed at Tanya's statement. Tasha concluded her experience by stating that her pair of Sean Paul glasses, deemed to be the only pair in existence, would have made her a millionaire from looking into the future of others.

Tanya (Miss Confused) had used her magic pen to erase her nickname and the fact that she came from a racist family, where the word 'nigger' was used frequently. This meant she had to develop secret friendships. She had also erased all the family members from her family tree who were known to use violence to feed their alter ego and to give off a strong message that blacks weren't welcome. She erased the day when a black boy had been stabbed in the head because of the colour of his skin, because she knew him. She erased the day she fell in love with a black boy because she was not allowed to love him.

'The Magic Land of Alice' experience had led Tanya to her own reality, which is where she stood with her magic pen erasing all the images that her version of 'The Magic Land of Alice' had projected. Little did she realise that she may have been erasing her reality but her strategies for dealing with that reality had not been erased, which is why she used the pen to draw herself as someone else, someone who had the courage to speak out. Tanya hoped that by doing this, her mouth would open to tell her family that diversity mattered.

Tanya had changed 'The Magic Land of Alice' experience in five seconds; it was no longer the bridge between reality and 'The Magic Land of Alice' where passages lead to a magical world of possibilities where you followed the carry on signs leading to your dream destination. A place where limitations were forbidden therefore it was limitless. Any outlaws found planting limitation seeds in the pathway of the traveller would be exiled from 'Alice Land'. Where the presence of colourful fairies would accompany you on your journey, encouraging you to explore hundreds of destinations because more than one existed, whilst chanting, whichever one you embraced the most would define you correctly and bring the gift of acceptance and internal happiness.

'Alice Land' had now morphed itself from a land of dreams and possibilities, to a land where secret passageways led to one destination, the destination of reality. Signs no longer said carry on. Instead, they told you to stop and witness yourself in the making. A place where limitation seeds were planted to prevent you from seeing beyond the experiences that you believed defined you.

CHAPTER 8

The Definition Game

A fter arriving back in the UK after a weekend of roach buts, late nights, erotic live sex shows, long walks down the coble streets of Amsterdam and having had developed an addiction for the Amsterdam space cake, they found themselves in the South terminal of Gatwick airport feeling rather exhausted.

As they walked through customs, they gave each other the eye. It was a secret code, asking whether any of them had brought anything back. All those who had walked before them insisted that if you were brave enough to bring cannabis back from Amsterdam, you were defined as a Don (Hero) and that upped your status in the Definition game.

The Definition game had dominated smudge life for as long as she could remember. The place that had limited everything (The Smudge) had produced a generation of hungry wannabes who were constantly searching for the way out, using the darkness to find the sunlight. Those she knew from the smudge were active players, all fighting and competing for the title and, depending on which Definition game you were playing or initiated into, determined the possibility of ever reaching it (The Don status)

The smudge had seen three deaths in the last twelve months because of the Definition game, where three young men had aspired to climb the Don hierarchy; all three deaths had the same outcome, but came from a different seed. The first seed planted was 'Greed' and had led to the death of one young man being shot in the back of his head ,for thinking that if he sold drugs on someone else's patch, should he Succeed, meant that he would achieve his one desire to be a Don. The second seed was 'Revenge", which led to the death of another young man because he lived in SE28. The boy that killed him was climbing the Don hierarchy of postcodes. The third young man died as a result of someone else wanting to take his Don title. All three were active players in the Definition game and it was known that those suspected of murder, one suspect had just turned sixteen.

She thought about how the media had a field day. It was no longer a crime of black and white that had dominated the media for decades. That had raised awareness of racial hatred extensively and became the reason why community groups were setting up protests against racism. For her, the Definition game had set up young people(with limited everything) on the road to nowhere, opening a gateway that gave the media an opportunity to feel their way through the darkness and into the sunlight, insisting that racial hate crime figures had dropped and introduce a new kind of crime. They called it black on black and linked it to the Definition game.

Passing through nothing to declare with the eye ball game still in play, they reached the arrival lounge and they all started laughing because they knew what the other one was doing. Joanne communicated, through her glaring eyeballs, that she had not brought anything back whilst Tanya said that she wished that she had. When asked why by Joanne, Tanya offered an exaggerated short story of how she wanted the DON status. The girls walked through the busy airport, laughing and joking, insisting that Tanya did not have what it takes to climb the DON Hierarchy and they once again found themselves in a passionate cussing session on the way to the taxi rank. The first taxi arrived and Tanya and Tasha got in. Before Tanya could close the taxi door, Joanne said "You know what happens to people who play the Definition game don't you, they either end up dead or they spend a lifetime searching". With that, Tanya and Joanne shared a short laugh and waved their goodbyes.

In the taxi with Joanne, Joanne used her jumper to rest her head on the car window and closed her eyes and slept. She looked out the window with her forehead touching the cold glass, reflecting on the three days in Amsterdam and feeling blessed that she had been finally been fed with another peak experience. She embraced each memory and added them to the photo book in her head. Looking out of the window and reflecting, she saw a motorway sign approaching and waited anxiously for it to get closer so she could see how long they had left to reach their destination. The motorway billboard reminded her of 'The Magic Land of Alice, except it gave you realistic destinations instead of dream destinations and even though Tanya had been responsible for the morphing of 'The Magic Land of Alice' she believed that it was still possible to return it back to its original state. She called this hope.

The motorway billboard was in her moment and it said fifty miles to London.

The Magic Land of Past

Her breath had created steam on the window of the taxi, so she drew a love heart. As the heart disappeared she drew it again and through the mist of her duplicated heart was 'The Magic Land of Alice'. She saw herself walking down the secret passage ways as she had done so many times before but the door at the end was locked. She stood there, frantically rattling the door handle. "It's me!" she cried, insisting the door open but there was no answer from the voice of 'The Magic Land of Alice'.

Looking confused she was forced to look around her environment for answers and it was then she noticed that this 'Magic Land of Alice' had only one door. In the silence she saw a small bundle of keys twinkling two feet from where she stood and she questioned if they were there for a reason. After some contemplation she picked them up and rolled them between her fingers, counting the number of keys that were attached to the ring that connected them all together. Whilst observing their movements as she rolled them between her fingers, she questioned which key would lead her to her destiny. Eventually, she chose a key. She inserted the key into the key hole of the locked door, turning it left and right and her heart started to flutter. But the key did not connect with the lock. Impatiently she tried another, then another, then another and she went through the whole bunch of keys until she came to the last one. It was the last key and it instantly connected to the lock and the door opened.

She pushed the door aggressively as if there was someone waiting to attack her from behind it and there she saw a long passage. It was dark and misty but clear enough for her to see a light flickering. Slowly she walked its path, her breath mixing with the mist as it left her mouth and she felt cold. Even so, she was drawn to the light. What she didn't notice was that as she walked, the path was morphing and changing its shape. She didn't notice this because her eyes were focused on the flickering light. Then, without warning the flickering stopped. She was already in the moment because the light had met her half way and it was then she saw the floating dust projections of herself.

(Projections can be received or given)

The dust projections were small dust particles that travelled together to project an image and once they were in the correct position, they would solidify. Her eyes followed the dust particles that were coming from all directions but she could not quite grasp the images because they were like thumb nail images. The dust projections came together and created an image that showed her the path she had already walked, floating and slotting into position as if one could not survive without the other. Creating a modern design and cleverly shaping an actual truth that told a story.

She watched in amazement and thought how clever and how powerful it was to see such a thing. As she watched, the images showed the first projection of how once she was defined as a warrior. This warrior had come together with forty thousand other warriors on the 16th of October 1993 to march against racism, where chants of "We are Black, we are White, together we are dynamite" echoing the streets of South east London. This was a time when racism was at its peak and this was a march protesting against the election of a BNP (British National Party) member, after there had been a recent racist attack on a young black boy who had been defined as promising student. This had followed the death of another promising young black male a few years before. He too had been black and beautiful.

She was a warrior who took to battle with bricks and bottles, alongside the other thirty-nine thousand warriors, as the first policeman took a swing for the young white warrior who was protesting on the front line, whilst thirty - nine thousand warriors stood behind him. She was a warrior who recognised that that day would be written in history because that day, thousands of people came together in black and white to unite.

The Re-Defining Process

The Projections that followed shaped and re shaped and now she realised that she was in 'The Magic Land of Past', the place that Tanya had given birth to, where pathways led to reality. She watched the projections unfold and it became clear that she had spent half of her life defining and then redefining herself like a flower that would open up and flourish, then close to redefine itself and open up again with a new sense of definition.

It was a process that would continue like an act of nature and regardless of how it opened, it was defined none the less. One projection had shown her how she had redefined herself in order to find love and finding love to her, defined her as being desirable, whether it was by one person or a few people.

The projections showed how she would define her facial features too with makeup, using an eye pencil to make her eyebrows more defined, lipstick to enhance her lips and eyeliner which made her eyes twinkle different shades of green. It had all been in the name of love. However the projections had also showed things he didn't like, causing her to redefine herself again. Another projection had shaped her peak experiences and she also witnessed earlier defining processes. It was evident that each projection had projected a truth, her truth. The truth was, she had spent all her life defining and redefining herself to gain respect, love and understanding and to her she believed these were the secret ingredients to acceptance in the way of definition.

She was woken up from 'The Magic land of Past' by the speed bump that lived at the end of her road. She was back in the heart of the smudge. She was home and it felt like it. It was a little mistier than usual, yet the block still looked like a clone, except the colour of the paint that had been used to paint its front doors. The abandoned tenants and special brew cans were still lying on their backs, nothing had changed.

She struggled out of the taxi half asleep and Joanne helped her to the lift, the lift that lived by itself on the ground floor. Joanne being Joanne dropped the bags and made a quick exit, making it clear she was not prepared to pay the taxi man for sitting down (what the car company defined as a waiting fee). She watched as Joanne got back into the taxi and Joanne sent her middle finger in the air, acting as if it were a sign of love.

Picking up the bags that were dumped by Joanne, she contemplated walking up the stairs to the third floor because she knew once that lift door opened, the smell of urine was going to make her vomit. Braving it out, she pressed the lift button and the lift door opened, she stepped in with every inch of her trying hard not to let any of her body touch the sides or breath in the strong smell of urine because she thought it contained acid particles that would singe out her lungs, should she be unfortunate enough to breath it in.

Running out of breath and her face straining whilst turning a funky pink, the lift doors opened and set her free from her two minute 'I'm a celebrity get me out of here' experience. She walked along the pathway to her front door, fondling in her pocket for her keys she eventually unlocked the front door to her one bedroom flat. In doing this, she had a sudden thought. Why couldn't unlocking the doors in her dreams be as easy as this? She could never grasp what dreams were or even if they meant anything. However, she knew she had gained something from this particular dream and that was the knowledge that she had spent half her life redefining herself.

The letters that had been posted over the weekend had created a mountain under her feet as she walked in and she sighed as if she was taking her last breath. Nothing had changed. It was as it had been before she had left and now she was the one conforming to the mission statement of the smudge, "I'm here, until the clouds lift, god willing". After dumping her bags similar to the way Joanne did, the feeling of feeling undefined began to suffocate her. The experience of the 'Magic Land of Past' as weird as she thought the dream was reinforced that once she had once been recognised in the world of definition.

CHAPTER 9

The Seed of Curiosity

Whilst she sat on the sofa in the lotus position looking at the time, she became curious. Curiosity was dangerous to her; it had often been the one thing that had left her dancing in hot water many times before. Her curiosity had caused a lot of problems for her. She had been chased by police, experimented with illegal drugs, withheld information in her head because it was safer and been led into dangerous situations. It was curiosity that had given her a good beating on more than one occasion by a gang of girls. Her curious nature seemed to live in her blood and her friends had often told her that her curiosity was going to kill her one day but back then she didn't give a shit and, to her, curiosity had been the key to adventure.

Her curiosity vibration was present, she could feel it. Even though it was only a little vibration, she knew that all it would take to make the vibration harder and stronger was to wake it up! The curiosity vibration had been sleeping ever since she left her peak experience but now she wanted to wake it. She wanted to wake it up because nothing made sense.

Now she felt more undefined than ever. It did not make sense that having had a place at one of London's top universities was not enough to earn a respectful place in the world. It did not make sense that a dream had provoked something new and it did not make sense why her daughter was not home yet.

As she waited for the return of her daughter, (she had received a text message to say they were running late), the curious vibration felt like it was sitting at the bottom of a bottomless pit. It was there and she knew it was but how far down in the bottomless pit it was, was unclear. She had visions of herself abseiling down this bottomless pit and forcing the curiosity to climb a few levels because there was something she wanted to know.

'The Magic land of Past' had created the curiosity and when her curiosity was in play she was like a bulldog with a bone. She had always responded to it in this way, hence why her curiosity, had made her delirious previously. She was curious to know how 'The Magic land of Past' worked. She wondered, if it is the place you go to walk pathways to your reality (past and present), If she knew how it worked there was a good possibility she could find the pathways to the future.

In her mind, pathways to the future would give her secret ingredient to the definition of self. This thought excited her. Had she found the secret ingredient that would enable her to define herself? Was this it? She could then manipulate 'The Magic Land of Past' to morph and show pathways to the future. And in doing so she believed she would be blessed with everything, acceptance of self, acceptance from others, a meaningful place in the world but more importantly living a life of internal happiness in the way of definition. She concluded that 'The Magic Land of Past' had provided her with a new form of powerful knowledge

She knew, how she was going to be defined in the future depended on if she knew how 'The Magic land of Past' worked. Her thought process had exceeded her expectations. She was adamant this time she was going to define herself and not live a life of others definition of her.

Her Curiosity was now climbing the bottomless pit, hungry to explore the possibilities of finding the definition of self and she knew exactly where to begin. It was at the beginning of two eras one old and one new. She knew in order to learn how 'The Magic Land of Past' worked she had to see it in action from the beginning and take notes, so she could learn and understand the formula it used, for her to successfully shape her future. She must then learn it and use the information in attempt to change the formula, manipulating it to show future pathways. She would then have the power to start at the beginning of a new era using the new formula to guide her to the definition of self.

This was a new era and she felt it. All those projections she saw had belonged to a different time in her life, what she was now calling the past and yesterday and with her curiosity climbing the bottom less pit. She was curious.

Finally her daughter had arrived and she embraced her for the first time in three days. As she hugged her she felt an overwhelming vibration of love and excitement. This is new, she thought. She loved her daughter of course but this was a deeper intense feeling of love that she believed had not been there before. Maybe this was the bond she had heard so much about, it had finally arrived. She remembered how people had spent most of her pregnancy telling her about this amazing bond that happens between a mother and child instantly after birth, but for her the instant bond everyone passionately talked about was not there when she had given birth. Instead she spent the first six months waiting for it. That was until she accepted that there was something wrong, because those around her insisted that if the bond they had spoken about was not there instantly after birth, that was a sign there was something wrong. It was something wrong that scared her and rather than question their definition she allowed the doctor to call it postnatal depression.

She embraced the bond that had finally arrived but at the same time questioned why it had taken so long. She spent a few seconds beating herself up about it and as she did, she reflected on her four years of motherhood, looking for answers or an explanation of how and why. Her new awakened curiosity now climbed another level. She was becoming curious about everything. She wanted to know why things happened to her, how she could stop them from happening and if what was happening defined who she was.

Her now awakened curiosity was climbing the bottom less pit and the vibrations were getting stronger. Curiosity was hungry and the higher he climbed the hungrier he became. His hunger became her hunger and now she was hungry and curious to learn how 'The Magic Land of Past worked'.

She pulled out a pair of small clogs; that she had brought back from her three day trip in Amsterdam and gave them to her daughter, who began pottering around the house. Unpacking clothes and creating childlike conversations with her daughter, who was now clogging around her one bedroom flat, laughing at the noise they made, she was happy to be home. She could feel curiosity's vibration whist she was washing up in the kitchen and she didn't know if she should be excited or fearful.

CHAPTER 10

Ingredient to the Soul

After a thousand soapsuds, ten plates, four cups and a soaking wet tea towel and after questioning how she was ever going to understand how 'The Magic Land of Past' worked, she turned on the music system in her living room. Music to her was magical. She called it the best doorway to her soul and her taste in music was very diverse and always reflected her mood. If she wanted to go back to an earlier time in her life, it would be what she called the classics from your Bel Biv Divoe's to your Limited additions. It was a time when swing had dominated the music lovers of that era. The times when she had felt stuck in a rut or was heartbroken, her R&B selection was guaranteed to leave her crying and feeling sorry for herself. And because he was another arsehole, she did have her selection of fuck you tracks that she played to empower herself into not giving a shit. The tracks that were produced by female artists who too had chosen arseholes and were going to use the arsehole to help them get a number one hit in the music charts. However the era of the 'Jungle Is Massive' is what she used to set her Tiger free and in doing so the Jungle vibration either did one of two things. Either it reinforced the fact she needed a night out or it made her aggressive and released the Gangster.

Pulling out a different CD because the one in the system kept jumping, she inserted a Prince CD titled 'Purple Rain'. The intro played and she could feel her dance vibration. She had been a dancer from the age of ten and it was being a dancer that had led her to 'The Magic Land of Alice', the place where the secret passageways told her that she was going to be a professional dancer for the Notorious B.I.G. The first track played and she was in her moment; singing and swaying. Her heart was truly open.

She listened, her heart listened and together they were dancing, embracing the beats and the words that brought the beats to life. The memories flowed; as did her soul and when she was bored of that she changed the CD. She thought how simple it would be if you could change your life in the same way you changed a CD, when life was shit or you felt as if you were on the path to nowhere, the simple changing of a CD would change your direction and you would follow the path because you knew it would lead to a place of honest, soulful music. A place that would be exciting brightly coloured with lots going on and a place where you would admit it was the place where you'd rather be.

The music stopped and so did the dance vibration because her daughter had turned it off. She always wondered how amazing it was that something as simple as music could bring a room to life and how on many occasions she had seen music send vibrations though many souls, often starting with the two step and always leading to a shake down. Music to her was like a magic spell, it always brought out the free will in people, the free will to explore the soul but she also knew how music could take you on many journeys in your head, where you would remember an era, a person or even where you were at that time.

Agreeing to watch a movie with her daughter, who was now bored of clogging around the living room and listening to music, she sat down on the sofa and positioned herself again in the lotus position. In the silence, other than the words that were projected from the television, her thoughts were now engaging in the last CD that she had played. The CD that she had waited ages for and involved a lot of begging. She called it her 'hands off' CD because every time she played it her friends would go crazy and asked to borrow it, which always ended in a no because she knew she was never going to get it back. It was general knowledge that lending out CD's of this calibre was a no no because those in the smudge had the tendency to pass it around, causing it to get lost in translation. The 'hands off' CD was one of four others that had replaced her original mixed tapes and with people getting pissed off, trying to un curl the brown tape that lived in the heart of the cassette, CD's were becoming more popular to music lovers around the world. Unless you were her Nan, who could never get to grips with the CD and therefore still used the tape deck, killing the neighbours with "Love Me Tender".

Venn had put the 'hands off' CD together, an aspiring DJ with an ear for music and everyone in the smudge knew him. Anytime anyone was having a party he was the man and if you didn't have Venn playing at your party, your party was going to be shit. He lived, breathed and dressed music, with his caps and jackets, forever making a statement and he spent a lot of his time doing music for people. Starting with the classic mixed tape then he too jumped on the CD bandwagon. If you had a CD or a mixed tape by Venn, then you were somebody.

She and Venn became friends because of Venn's close friendship with her brother. Venn and her brother were always knocking around the smudge; checking girls and jumping on what was known as, the 272 bus route to nowhere with the rest of the 272 massive.

The 272 massive were a group of friends who had all grown up in the smudge. All had their individually picked names, from your Chip Pan's to your Andre's. A lively group of young boys who congregated together like a mass of energy, all embraced the testosterone that filled the 272 bus and had what they called a bungling session. BUNGLE! This always lead to the boys jumping on top of each other until there was a mountain of boys, shouting, laughing and screaming as if they were fighting over the one girl who existed in the bottom of the pile. This kind of activity on the 272 bus had always resulted in the police being called by the frightened bus driver who had not yet kept himself up to date with the changes in the testosterone levels being projected by the new generation of young men.

She remembered that era for the BUNGLE being at the heart of the brotherhood and then, girls started creating sisterhoods, jumping on the 272 bus route and having bungling sessions of their own. She believed that her teenage years allowed her to define herself. There were no high expectations and there were only ever two rules on the agenda; don't be late and turn up for school. The society in which she lived allowed her to make mistakes and be a little lost. It was what youth workers used to call 'the adolescent's process', giving teenagers the right to fuck up and when they were asked why, adolescence gave them a pass called the 'I don't know' card.

Definition to her then, largely depended on who was doing the defining and who was asking. Her impulsive behaviour was the secret ingredient that defined her during earlier years, which is why she had spent most of it being a part of a sisterhood, running from police, stealing from shops and beating up girls from different postcodes. She had also been beaten up many a time. But the best thing she remembered about her teenage years was the constant competition with the brotherhood and she called it the battle of the testosterone levels.

Music was not only the doorway to her soul, it was the doorway to the past and whilst sitting in the lotus position with her new thoughts for company, it became clear she had redefined herself several times between the ages of thirteen and nineteen like a Rubik's cube showing its different sides. She recalled redefining herself to suit friends' expectations, her parent's expectations, society's expectations and the expectations of the opposite sex. However, by the time she reached eighteen and whilst having her unknowingly last peak experience, she had noticed there had been a shift. She had noticed that the society in which she lived expected a different definition of her and this one did not include impulsive behaviour. They expected more which is why they called it adulthood

CHAPTER 11

The Answers Always in the Question

It had been a few days since she had returned from her Amsterdam experience and her curiosity had climbed all ten levels of the bottom less pit. His paws were sore and his coat was dirty but he was out and he was hungry. The music experience had given her the key to learn how 'The Magic Land of Past' worked and music was the secret ingredient that triggered her autobiographical memory. The autobiographical memory is what she referred to as the photo book in her head but it was not just a photo book. It was also a diary that provided detailed information about her and her past experiences, which came from her episodic memory. Her episodic memory was how she was able to link music to her past experiences and translate it into where, when and how, all of which tapped into her emotional matrix.

She used the three secret ingredients (Music, autobiographical and episodic) to try and unlock 'The Magic land of Past' and she started at the beginning. Well, as far back as the autobiographical memory would let her. Using all three secret ingredients, she walked the path of her reality from the beginning, took notes and tapped into her emotional matrix until she believed she had the formula to 'The Magic Land of Past'.

This was not the first time she had an autobiographical experience. She had encountered it before at different times in her life. Sometimes it was triggered through music, sometimes triggered through a movie, event or a place that reminded her that she had already been there or done it. However, this time she was embracing it because she knew that in order to find the pathways to the future she needed to know how 'The Magic Land of Past' worked.

Unfortunately for her, whilst trying to understand how 'The Magic Land of Past' worked she came to realise her the autobiographical memory is also what helps us to create a sense of self and when for some reason that does not happen, it can trigger a negative response, hence why at one point in her life, she had been sliding down the kitchen wall, threatening to cut her wrists during her episode of derangement and the reason why she was now angry, emotional and looking for someone or something to blame.

Pathways to the Future

Her curiosity had found the formula by using all three ingredients and with the calibration of all three working together, she understood the formula to 'The Magic Land of Past'. But even after months of painful note taking, reliving the experiences and trying to control her emotional matrix, she was only a quarter of the way into the understanding the shaping of 'The Magic Land of Past'. Even so, she had the formula. The formula helped to understand how it worked and she believed it would be only a matter of time before she understood the shaping. The shaping of 'The Magic land of Past' was important; it is at the heart of 'The Magic Land of Past' behaviour pattern. Behaviour patterns are 'key' in shaping pathways.

Her autobiographical memory and her episodic memory had been successful in providing her with new information. She had leant that she could not control 'The Magic Land of Past, but now she had the formula, she could manipulate it. She also gained a better understanding of how 'The Magic Land of Past' shaped itself and depending on how it behaved determined the pathways that were created. Now she had the enhanced feeling that she wanted to find the definition of self, but under no circumstances did she want to be defined in the same the way 'The Magic Land of Past' had defined her previously.

She no longer wanted to give a man's dick the power to define her. Instead, she wanted to treat her body as a temple. She no longer wanted to take Class A drugs or smoke cannabis because oblivion was not a place she liked. She no longer wanted her impulsive behaviour to be her dictator just because the outcome was never the same. She no longer wanted the feeling that her soul had been taken because she had allowed people to take it. She no longer wanted the society in which she lived to make the rules, because they were rules of oppression. She no longer wanted to be attached to the labels because she had not even written them. She no longer wanted to be in the benefit trap because she no longer wanted to belong to a herd. She no longer wanted the words of others to hurt because it made her live up to their expectations and she no longer wanted to be someone who felt undefined because being undefined meant that you did not have a respectful place in the world.

She was now manipulating the formula belonging to 'The Magic land of Past' to show pathways to the future. The experience had taught her many things and had also taught her about the freedom of choice. From mastering how 'The Magic Land of Past' worked she had a revelation and it was simple, there was no truth in the mission statement of the smudge, it had nothing to do with the cards she was dealt, it had everything to do with the choices she made.

The peak experiences had not defined her; it was the choices she made within the experiences that had defined her. She had chosen to belong to a sisterhood in her earlier years. She had chosen not to give a shit. She had chosen to party and take drugs and she had chosen her friends. She had chosen for her impulsive behaviour to become her dictator and she had chosen to have unprotected sex during her unknowingly last peak experience. It was the power of choice that had defined her, once she was pregnant there was no choice and it was not having the choice that had given birth to the feeling of feeling undefined.

If it had not been for the bravery of a defined warrior, willing to explore 'The Magic Land of Past' to understand how it worked, she would have been none the wiser. She would have continued her journey like those living in the smudge; living amongst the clouds and having limited everything, still believing it had everything to do with the cards you were dealt. But the real revelation was the knowledge of choice and how powerful choices were in shaping pathways and it was this that morphed 'The Magic Land of Past' to 'The Land of Possibilities'.

She was now feeling awake and educated. She joined all the A's, B's and C's like the spaghetti junction but this time she had the answers. It was because she had been forced out of her peak experiences that she had felt undefined, which lead to her to 'The Magic Land of Past' which had showed her that she had once been a warrior. It was her curiosity climbing the bottomless pit, which had led to the beginning of the questioning of everything and it was her determination to find the definition of self, which was born out of the feeling of being undefined.

Now, she was facing her fears and opening her mind to experiment and manipulate the world she lived in. It was all in the name of the definition of self. Wow, she thought, with an ABC like that, being defined in this world is paramount to her existence.

CHAPTER 12

The Search for the Definition of Self

Youth worker, Care worker, Prison officer, Community officer, Crime prevention, Drugs worker were some of the endless definition titles amongst the endless job application forms she had spent four weeks completing.

To her it was like ground hog day; waking up and questioning if you were waking up, again in the morning of Tuesday and having to check the calendar to make sure that there had been an actual transition from Tuesday to Wednesday. The number of rejection letters reinforced what she already knew. Clearly attending London's top university was not enough to be defined and change her definition from unemployed to employed. To top it all off, it looked as if employers were also jumping on the 'not-quite-good-enough' bandwagon, as most rejection letters stated that if you wanted to know why you were not good enough, you could give them a call.

She did not understand the world she lived in. Its formula did not make sense. She thought that when people said "the whole worlds gone mad" what they were actually talking about was, how can a world with so many rules and a world known to be obsessed with definition, where everything that existed within it was defined, make the pathways to the definition of self, so complicated. How was it possible that those had done everything to give them something in the way of definition to prove they had earned a respectful place in the world, were still not being recognised and even worse by a world who claims definition is paramount to ones existence?

She began to feel rather bitter. You put your arse through university against all the odds, to gain the qualifications to do the work and then the work tells you, experience is what they are looking for. No one at the London's top university had stated that this was the case. They had insisted that it was the qualification that defined you and it was the key to earning a respectful place in the world.

She did not see the challenges that lay between her and the definition of self. She did not recall any challenges during her visits to 'The Magic Land of Alice' because it was a place that was limitless and 'The Magic Land of Past' could be manipulated. Now her curiosity was roaming the grounds searching for something and that something was a loop hole. She knew that should she find it, she was most definitely going to jump through it and its flames of fire.

After eight weeks, a hundred rejection letters and still searching for the definition of self, she had found the loop hole. She had obtained herself a part time job as a Care Assistant working with hard to reach young people. Chance had put out the flames so she could jump through the loop hole without getting burnt. Chance had earned herself a full time position at an organisation that was set up to work with young people who were in care, having been removed from the family home as a result of a parent with an addiction.

Chance had previously stated that she had got the job, not because of her qualification, but because of her life experience. Being the daughter of a heroin addict had defined her as the ideal employee for she had what they liked to call 'experience'. Chance claimed that experience outweighed the old testament (when qualifications defined you as being good enough). Endless research echoed that those with life experience not only gave more but improved the quality of work delivered by services. Now, organisations were trying to figure out how 'The Magic land of Past' worked so they too could manipulate their own pathways to providing better services in the future.

Having obtained a job that defined her as a Care Assistant; her badge was something that she could show to the world to prove she had earned a respectful place within it, which is why she always wore it on the outside for the world to see.

The Redefining Process in 3D

Twelve months had passed and she was bored with her title and felt that it had passed its sell by date. In twelve months, she had been surrounded by colleagues who were constantly searching for the gateways to promotion. The more they wanted it, the more hours they did and the more hours they did, the more they brown nosed the bosses who had the key to the next level of definition, and she wanted it .

The Care Assistant role became an embarrassment rather than something she wanted to show to the world, hence why, after six months she tucked it neatly in her top and was now questioning as to why something that had defined her in the beginning and gave her some form of internal happiness, did not define her anymore. She wanted more and to get more she needed to do more and in doing more she believed she would find the endless definition of self. (Endless definition, a strategy used to replace the definition of self). She believed that in achieving more, she could earn a more respectful place in the world. Now she was the one with an addiction because she was addicted to finding the endless definition of self. It was now a game of chase.

She chased the Care Officer promotion which defined her as an arse licker, back stabber and caused people to stop talking when she walked in the room, but she didn't give a shit. She was at her peak, shaping her pathways to the future in hope that the pathways would lead to the endless definition of self. Being at your peak is doing whatever, wherever and to whom ever and not giving a shit.

Her ability to manipulate the formula and adapt the behaviour pattern that shaped her pathways was how she had been successful in getting the promotion. The one promotion ten other people desired. She understood how the system worked and how to change her behaviour to get what she wanted. The definition as a Care Assistant to her was not the endless definition of self. It was an imposter who, for six months, had led her to believe it was an endless definition. However, she had earlier life experiences in recognising verbal diarrhoea and the 'Care Assistant' badge was full of it.

She didn't notice the verbal diarrhoea that flowed from the title that projected itself through the plastic, until people told her: you can't do this, you can't do that, you are not qualified to do so and it's not in your job description. She was afraid of being returned to the darkness, where she once had held that undefined feeling, so she chose to define those unsuccessful candidates as jealous bitches who hated the fact that she had what it took to shit on everyone and everything thing to feed her addiction to finding the endless definition of self .

In her new role, she was a worker who produced results and the mangers knew it, the workers knew it, the young people knew it and she knew it too. Again she was living up to the expectations of others and pushing herself to live up to the definition she had been given, its set of rules and labels she had not even written. The labels stated that to be defined as being an outstanding Care Officer you must do the following: have no compassion when it came to your colleagues, accept that now your own children are latch key children because the job comes first, go in when you're sick, get someone else to look after your children when they are sick, work half terms and summer holidays and tell people they need to attend training because they are defined as not being quite good enough.

You had to tell your family if they wanted you to earn a respectful place in the world, they had to understand that you are unavailable from Monday to Friday (and that includes most half terms and summer holidays). But more importantly, they needed to know that looking after other people's children is what you do and you will continue you to do it because that is what defines you. It pays the bills, keeps a roof over your head in the heart of the smudge and also pays for two weeks in the Caribbean. These two weeks, out of the five weeks (defined as holiday) that had been allocated to spend time with your own children, spent in the Caribbean meant you had earned a respectful place in the world.

Her addiction to finding the endless definition of self was now shaping her pathways, so much so she became addicted to titles and salaries. The Care Officer title no longer defined her in the way she wished, so she changed her job. This change brought with it another definition with a similar set of rules and when she felt she was heading to the darkness, she redefined herself into another job role with a similar set of rules, causing her addiction to crave the pathways to something better. And each time she craved better, it came at a price. Choice was no longer shaping her pathways because to say 'No' to working on bank holidays, half terms and summer holidays did not define you as being committed.

Her addiction to obtain the endless definition became her new dictator and in redefining herself in the game of chase, her addiction had given birth to selfishness, and impulsive behaviour. Her addition had allowed her soul to be taken and allowed society to continue to make the rules. It had given life to her past too because now her own daughter was experiencing neglect and claimed that she felt neglected from Monday to Friday, some bank holidays, half terms and summer holidays. It was all in the name of the endless definition of self. She believed it was paramount to her existence and that's why she had developed the disease, the same decease that affects thousands of people who too are searching. Especially women, whose fight to find a definition was a battle of the testosterone level, in the psychological institution known as work. After all, they were living and working in an endless definition, defined as a man's world.

CHAPTER 13

Recognising the Warrior

During her career, whilst being addicted to titles and salaries and still searching for the endless definition of self, she realised that young people too were striving to be defined in order to find a respectable place in the world.

In striving for their own version of definition, they were defined as dysfunctional and rebellious but to her they were a mirror image of her earlier experiences. Because of this, she had developed a good working relationship with each of them. She recognised their frustration and confusion and what cloned them together were similar life experiences.

They too had been given the 'I don't know' card every time they fucked up but luckily for them, the society in which they lived still allowed them to make mistakes for it still had low expectations of the new generation of wannabes. That was until they reached eighteen, when she knew the world's definition of them would change to one that did not include impulsive behaviour. They were still calling it adulthood. She embraced all the rebellious behaviour and read between the lines. In doing so, it triggered the photo book she kept in her head and she used the photo book as a form of exchange. It worked as an exchange of you tell me yours and I'll tell you mine.

Young men were still fighting the DON hierarchy and the seeds of Greed, Revenge and Titles were still being planted into the virgin minds of these young men. Young girls were still striving to create sisterhoods, having peak experiences and attempting to make themselves, desirable to the opposite sex. It was now clear why Desire had led her into the field of community work. He knew that she had the tools and the life experience to show young people that 'The Magic land of Past' existed and could be manipulated. That choice was a powerful tool in shaping the pathways to the future. It was her knowledge and her passion that had defined her as a woman who had successfully empowered the lives of many young people, jumping into their souls to walk a thousand miles in their shoes and speaking of the world through her eyes to show young people what choice looked like. As a result she was given the Care Officer of the year award. However, her daughter would be the last to give her an award for the mother of the year. Her daughter now defined her as someone who had neglected her and had voiced, many a time, that her mothers addiction to finding the endless definition of self had made her no better than the woman she had tried so hard not to be. The mirror had presented itself as it had before and she was now staring her past in the face.

It had been a while since she had sensed The Shadow Self but she was now sensing his vibration and she knew for her to be sensing his vibration, she must have been lost. She questioned how she had ended up here after following the pathways to the future. Even though she had not found the endless definition of self, she was defined. Of course it had involved a lot of redefining, but to her she was defined none of the less. Having a successful career path is what she believed defined her and now her emotions began roaming to the place of 'nothing I do is good enough'. It is the place where everyone goes to get down on their knees and beg for things to make sense. It is where the autobiographical and the episodic memory works overtime, trying to figure it out and it is also a place you go to beat yourself up because yet again you have been defined as getting it wrong.

How far was it to the endless definition of self?, how will I know I am there? And where does internal happiness live? She could now hear the voice of The Shadow Self whispering, "You were so busy searching for the endless definition of self, you lost your way. You have forgotten what I taught you and unless lessons are learnt, your past will mirror your present". He then went on to say all the negative things that had led to her emotions roaming the place of 'nothing I do is good enough'.

The Reconnection with Self

Whilst sitting in the lotus position on a Saturday morning, she began reflecting with The Shadow Self for company. He had returned from the matrix where he had been living for the past six years. She had listened to him for the past three days since the word 'neglect' had flowed from her daughters lips. She was not sure if she had asked for The Shadow Self to return from the matrix or if he just turned up. Either way, she was not happy.

She was not happy because for the first time in six years she felt lost. She had followed the pathways to the future after killing herself to understand how 'The Magic Land of Past' worked and even though she felt defined as a successful career woman who had received acceptance from the world, who was now able to define her in a positive way, she was now asking herself what was the point. It was "what was the point" that her curiosity started to vibrate, vibrate as it had done before. Her curiosity eyes were wide open, whilst he floated in the air where she had left him during her addiction to finding the endless definition of self. For, it was her relationship with Desire who accompanied her in the game of chase.

During her reflection, the more she thought and the more she listened to 'The Shadow Self', the more she remembered how once she had thought he had stalker tendencies. She laughed to herself because in six years he had not changed. He quickly responded to that thought and made it very clear that it was not his purpose to change. This led her to ask him what was her purpose and expressed how she felt lost, (not undefined) but lost and she knew she was lost because the mirror had shown her she was. Her daughter had shown her the mirror of past and it was proof that history was somehow repeating itself and now the mirror was stalking her too. Her confusion jumped a brain cell whilst looking to him for answers and he stated that exploring her purpose was not his domain.

The phone rang. It was Joanne. Joanne had become like the sister she had always wanted and it was the projection of Joanne's middle finger that had bonded them together. She and Joanne shared everything and they were known to have the ideal friendship. They empowered each other to conquer the world. Both of them were searching for the endless definition of self and they always bitched about how yet another pathway had not led them to it. Joanne often stated that the endless definition of self did not exist because there was no one that she knew who had acquired it. She had always told Joanne, that was because those who hadn't acquired it didn't have the skills and because she and Joanne had been brought up in the smudge, they were more streetwise than most. Therefore, their noses were more likely to smell it.

To her, their noses were made to smell success. They had been brought up with limited everything and being brought up with limited everything made you more determined to train your noise. Joanne always laughed at the thought that she'd always referred to noses as pendulums to smell out pathways that led to success. Because her theory was never right in Joanne's case, Joanne would insist that she blew her nose more than often, with the hope that one day her nose would be on point. During the conversation, Joanne insisted again that the endless definition of self did not exist and to prove it, she wanted them to go and see a tarot reader. Joanne explained that it would be fun and could provide the answers to the mystery of how far they had to walk to find the endless definition of self, should it exist and whether they would be lucky enough to find where internal happiness lived. Joanne suggested it might even help to rebuild the relationship with her daughter; after all they had tried everything else.

The Two Faced Definition

After believing that she had done everything to find the endless definition of self and now feeling lost because the word 'neglect' had made her shudder, she and Joanne both turned up to a little shop in South East London that was built from books and crystals. As they walked in, Joanne starting laughing, expressing how interesting the experience was going to be. "If this shit is real and a stranger can tell me my past, present and future, I'll wear a dress for a day", Joanne said. Even though she laughed at Joanne's statement, she became anxious and she was now asking herself was this the place to get the answers? Did she want to relive the past, talk about the present or even want to know about the future? She had to ask herself why she was even there?.

The books that were stacked on the bookshelves made her even more anxious with their strange titles: 'The Secret', '5000 magic spells to get the life you want', 'The Magic' and 'The book of numerology' were just some of the titles. There were hundreds of books about power and how to obtain it. Whilst scanning the books with her eyes like an electronic bar code reader, her curiosity's vibration became stronger as she scanned the pages of a book called 'The Secret'. Curiosity's eyes were wide open and he saw dollar signs when she scanned the complicated ingredients for a money spell in the book of spells. She smiled as it had been the first time ever that she had experienced such books. No way does this stuff work, she thought. Even so, she appreciated that whoever had written the books had a great mind and a very extensive imagination.

Her name was called and she climbed a short stair case which led to a landing with two doors. It would have been like walking into a real life version of 'The Magic Land of Alice', had the experience been about her dreams but the era of 'The Magic Land of Alice' was truly over and had been since her Amsterdam experience. However she now questioned whether adulthood had something to do with it and all that remained was 'The Magic Land of Past'. She believed she had exhausted 'The Magic Land of Possibilities' from being a successful career woman. She took deep breaths and sat down at the table in the room where a lady had beckoned her. She heard Joanne's voice say "hello" to the tarot reader that was in the next room. She heard the door shut and she was now in the tarot reader's moment.

The room was quiet and a cent of lavender danced in the air. Facing her was a native Indian woman with long brown hair and blond highlights. The woman gave her name with conviction. Her name was

Destiny. Destiny asked for her name, her date of birth and for her to choose a colour, whilst insisting the colour should be the first one that came into her head, preventing it from going through the thought process. Well that's easy, she thought. It was very rare anything went through her thought process, hence why her mouth disease was very much present. "Here were go". In her head, she began mocking the woman's name and questioning how ironic it was that the tarot readers name was Destiny, whilst closing down her mind and closing all the doors to her soul and her open wounds, should the tarot reader be the real thing. There was silence in the room and while Destiny began working her magic; writing on paper and constructing tables with numbers and drawing lines through them, she could feel the sweat forming in the palms of her hands. She felt powerless. She knew that no matter what, it was coming. She was going to hear it and she was going to hear it today. She braced herself and strapped herself in tight with the invisible seatbelt she was now using to keep herself safe during this rollercoaster ride.

The first words that flowed from Destiny's lips were "You are looking for answers". She continued. "You have mastered 'The Land of Past' to change your future so you could be defined by the world as someone who had earned a respectful place with in it, yes?" She nodded her head. "Ah! It was a gift given to you from God and you will continue to use it in the future. You must be brave and face your deepest fears. The unknown is what will free you and shape your future for the better".

She was not impressed. She wanted more proof. That statement had been too general because to her, everyone was searching for answers, had a past and craved better in the future. She wanted to grill Destiny. In her head she had brief internal conversations with herself. She willed Destiny to give her something better, something to prove this was real.

"I can take it! I can take whatever it is you are going to say", she said to herself. At the same time she predicted that it was going to be her negative attributes that where going to flow from Destiny's mouth and slap her in the face. I am ready to hear the truth, see the unknown and where I went wrong, is what she was thinking, whilst preparing for her emotions to visit the place of 'nothing I do is good enough'.

Destiny went on: "Be confident in your decisions, for it is this that will help you find what you are searching for. At the moment you search for a myth that we all desire because if we think we have it, we believe we are better people and we cannot be judged". Destiny then went on to say; "There are two definitions of self, one internal and one external and you have been so busy with the external, projecting what you want people to see, you have forgotten the internal and it is the internal where you have failed. The internal is more powerful than the external and if you want to really know who you truly are, you need to explore the internal treasures that exist in your internal caves. Only then will you be truly blessed and live the life you so desire". Destiny ended her version of the truth with, "The external and internal is known as the definition of two faces. Confused.Com or what! She had no idea what the hell Destiny was talking about. Internal caves? She questioned what they were.

She sighed with the thought of how she had spent £30 in desperation looking for answers, answers deemed to her, as way out there. She knew that if she told anyone of her visit to the tarot reader and what had been said, her friends, if not her family, would most defiantly be hushing her off to put her in a strait jacket if she even mentioned that she believed. Even so she now desired the answers from Destiny. Her main desire was how to address the situation with her daughter because Destiny was now being defined as someone who could possibly see what she could not.

It was then Destiny asked her to shuffle the cards and ask a question. She split the pack into three piles and one after the other Destiny flipped the cards, making a cross shape on the table in front of her. This astounded her because the method that Destiny was using to read the tarot cards was the same method that 'The Magic Land of Past' used whist shaping the dust projections. Presented, in a shape and connecting to one another.

"Your daughter needs more time. Stop chasing something that does not exist because it has taken you away from something that is important to you. For too long your addiction has created something you did not want to happen. Your daughter is still young and therefore forgiving. You need to explore your internal caves and it is here you will truly find what it is you have been searching for."

Was this experience possible and how would it be possible? How could a stranger and a bunch of cards have given her the solution to address the neglect that flowed from her daughters lips? Even though she could not make sense of the internal caves, she believed. She did not know why she believed but she did and as her tarot reading was coming to an end after thirty minutes of what she called a rollercoaster, Destiny gave a profound statement.

"Even though the endless definition of self does not exist, the numerous job roles and people perceptions are an endless definition of self in itself. As long as you are employed and labelled you will be defined endlessly, my dear." With that, Destiny smiled and wished her good luck.

CHAPTER 14

The Land of Possibilities

Whilst waiting for Joanne to finish her tarot reading, she walked around the shop in awe of the books and the crystals and came across a book called 'What's in a Name'. She shook her head, begging for her curiosity to close his eyes because the thought of having to follow new pathways, which she assumed were to do with the internal caves that Destiny was ranting about, gave her a headache. She knew her version of the endless definition of self did not exist, not because Destiny had stated that was the case, but because at some point she realised that as her experiences changed so did she. It was not rocket science. It was like knowing Father Christmas does not exist when you get to a certain age, but you still get excited and put out the cookies and milk because you want to believe and that has everything to do with the magic it brings into the souls of thousands of people.

The finding of the endless definition of self was more to do with believing in the magic of finding internal happiness and putting a stop to the redefining process. Finding it would mean that it was then ok to stop searching. Ok to no longer demand the answers and that she no longer had to prove she had earned a respectful place in the world, as a result she would give the gift of time. No longer searching would have caused the world to slow down and move in slow motion. It would be slow enough for her to see the world, embrace the experience, see the lesson, embrace the people, see her family and capture all of it. Capturing it meant never missing a unique opportunity which would allow you to embrace the growth of those around you, see a crisis and offer to help because time would be moving slow enough to see it. You could embrace conversations into the night to discover the things you never knew and conquer the world in your own time.

She wished for a world without definition because she wanted to experience it. She wished for a world that moved slowly enough so she had the time to teach people the truth; that life had nothing to do with the cards you were dealt, but everything to do with the choices you made. Time would be the gift that allowed people to question everything and look deeper into the meaning of life and question if definition was something that was man made to distract you from what was really going on in the world?.

As her brain ticked away whilst she walked around the shop, examining the books and crystals, she found herself once again in the lift belonging to Mr Willy Wonker. Suddenly, in awe of the incense that was now dancing up her nose, she felt a calm she had not experienced before. She was still, in the silence of the book shop and she sensed a new vibration, one with so much feeling she could not put it into words. It was extraordinary, that vibration had led her to slow down her mind, her thoughts and herself and now she was in her own moment.

She questioned if what she was experiencing was inner peace but she had not experienced it before so she didn't know. Besides, it was highly unlikely because she associated inner peace with those who went to church to repent their sins. Along with those who had claimed to have been sent here to do Gods work and it was God's work that woke her up every Sunday morning thanks to Jehovah. She had so much baggage defined as issues; there was no space or room for inner peace. Although she was not spiritual, and far from it, she found herself standing in this small shop built from books and crystals, experiencing a slow moment.

A slow moment that made her realise external had no meaning and meant nothing. She knew it meant nothing because she had seen those with nothing project nothing but internal happiness. Where the words, "we have nothing but we are internally grateful and internally happy with the blessings we do have" flowed from their lips. She recalled television adverts showing children smiling in some of the worst poverty areas in Africa, even though they had not eaten or drunken clean water for days. But those, like her, who had everything because of their addition to finding the endless definition of self (that helped to numb the soul during the search), were stressed, tired, unhappy and their emotions often visited the place of " nothing I do is good enough" is where her slow moment ended.

Still looking and waiting, she read the back of the books, she read the front, she put them down, she picked them up and the woman at the front desk was watching. Why is it that when you're in a shop for too long, the eyes of fixation find themselves on the back of your head? Instantaneously, she defined the woman as an irritating bitch and carried on looking.

Eventually, Joanne came down the stairs, raised her eyebrows and pulled out her bottom lip. They looked at each other in suspense, paid their bill and left the shop. Outside the shop, one lit a cigarette and the other lit a spliff and together they stood there puffing away, one into oblivion and the other into a place of stability. They walked around the corner from the shop built from books and crystals and as Joanne was walking with a bounce in her step, like a clone of Danny Zuko, she fondled in her pocket for her car keys. Joanne pulled the keys out from her coat pocket, pressed the button and the car doors opened at the sound of the beep and they got in the car.

The car did not move and continued to not move for thirty five minutes, they were far too busy giving their interpretation of events to each other to care. Whilst one done the talking, the other did the dissecting and eventually when Joanne had returned from the place called oblivion, she inserted the key into the ignition and put her foot on the accelerator, leaving the small shop built out of books and crystals behind.

CHAPTER 15

Recognising Change

After arriving in the car park in the heart of the smudge after continuous talking and dissecting, Joanne pointed out the window to a red Audi convertible sitting on its four wheels with its neon number plate that read MT02 HOTT. Tasha (Miss Hotness to the Universe and to all men) was moving around the car like a mad woman, waving her arms about as usual. They could not work out if Tasha was on her mobile phone having a chaotic moment or whether she was dancing to the tunes that were escaping from the small gap in the window. She and Joanne started laughing and made a pact not to mention where they had just been. As they got out the car, Tasha (Miss Hotness to the Universe and to all men) spotted them and wound down her car window, waving her arms about whilst shouting that she had been calling them for the past ten minutes and where the hell had they been.

Joanne walked past Tasha's car, eyeballing the neon number plate and smirking. "Really Tasha?"

Tasha (Miss Hotness to the Universe and to all men) turned off her CD player and got out the car. She pulled the driver's seat forward whilst cursing and shouting. Out stepped two children, Divan her little boy and Savannah her little girl, both aged two. In Tasha's arms was six week old Tiffany. Three years had seen Tasha (Miss Hotness to the Universe and to all men) continue to have many peak experiences after the Amsterdam experience and when Tasha had first got pregnant with twins two and a half years ago, it was Tanya who had insisted that Tasha should have used her magic pen to draw herself a real pair of Sean Paul's glasses. Tasha was still living in the end house where the smudge did not quite reach; her parents had moved out and had a luxury villa in the South of France. Tanya now lived in their house and had no idea where her sister was.

Tasha (Miss Hotness to the universe and to all men) was now a part of a herd thanks to her two baby fathers who had both disappeared and now Tasha had to face the truth. Tasha had chosen to have unprotected sex with her sister's boyfriend. This had led to Tasha losing a sister but gaining twins. It had also led to her parents having to buy her a car and move out so Tasha had somewhere to live.

Tasha's choices gave her a more permanent place in the benefit trap. This set her on the pathway to boredom and was why Tasha had Tiffany six weeks ago. Even so, Tasha believed it was the cards that she had got dealt because her pathways did not lead to 'The Magic Land of Past'. Tasha did not question anything nor demand the answers, which is why she had no interest in manipulating her pathways to the future. Tasha had not experienced the feeling of being undefined, so therefore she did not develop an addiction to search for the definition of self. However what did define Tasha was a man's dick and she had told the girls that as long as she had a man, she was happy. Tasha desired nothing more and even though neither of her baby fathers were around, it was only a matter of time before she allowed another man's dick to define her and inject another form of internal happiness inside her.

They waited for the lift on the ground floor, Tasha and her three children were now the ones dreading the lift and as the lift door opened the smell of urine made their eyes water. Even though Tasha's life had changed dramatically because of her own addiction to men, Tasha still thought she was Miss Hotness to the Universe and to all men. Tasha was no longer a size eight, no longer wore high heels and no longer visited the '£10 a full set' nail shop, hence why Joanne was smirking at Tasha's neon number plate, MT02 HOTT. Joanne no longer defined Tasha as HOTT.

Climbing the stairwell where the special brew and the cans of tenants were still lying on their backs looking rather abandoned, she and Joanne met Tasha on the third floor of the building that was still acting like a clone in the heart of the Smudge. The only changes that had happened over the past few years were the new windows that looked like clones of each other as well. They helped Tasha with her two eldest children, because after five minutes in the lift Tasha looked like she wanted to vomit. She admitted that she was too posh to walk and whilst laughing at Tasha's 'too posh to walk' statement, they found something more amusing to laugh at; Tasha's hair had Tiffany's vomit in it. It was clear that the major change in Tasha was that she no longer freaked out at the sign of shit or the other things that were an act of nature.

Change had affected all three of them. Joanne was no longer angry because angry defined her as being hard to work with and with her desire for wanting to work in the studio and produce music with likeminded people; she chose to seek counselling to address her anger issues. This had led to her being head hunted in the music industry and she was now defined as a promising music producer. Tasha (Miss Hotness to the Universe and to all men) no longer lived the life of Miss Universe and everyone recognised the change in her because she no longer projected what she wanted others to see. This was because she was too tired and too busy raising three children on her own. Men no longer wanted to leave their girlfriends for her because she was defined as someone who had two different baby fathers and a woman who had not only slept with Arthur but had slept with half of South East London. Woman like Tasha were seen to have no dreams or aspirations, therefore they were now being defined as being unattractive to men in the year of the Millennium.

Change had seen Tanya into Holloway Prison, serving a three year sentence for growing cannabis in two large tents to the value of £6000. This had been two and a half years ago. The C on her neck had been a sign that she had started climbing the DON hierarchy and it was a sign she had been initiated into a notorious gang based in North London, prior to the Amsterdam experience. In every letter Tanya wrote she now defined herself as someone who's soul had been taken because to stop herself from getting beaten up each day for refusing to crutch drugs that were passed to her from someone on a visit from the outside, she had to find herself a girlfriend who was hard enough to protect her. But it also meant that the sex was a bit rough, hence why on every prison visit the girls were presented with new gash marks down Tanya's arms, accompanied with a variety of bruises.

As for her, change had led her to the shop built out of books and crystals and was the reason why she was still questioning. Change had led to the fireball she was now holding in her emotional matrix of guilt because if it had not been for her addiction to defining herself, sending her on the search for her version of the endless definition of self, to show she had earned a respectful place in the world, the word 'neglect' may not have flowed from her daughter lips.

CHAPTER 16

Going through the Changes

After a long drawn out visit from Tasha and her three screaming little treasures, defined as children, she and Joanne began writing a joint letter to Tanya. It was important to both of them that it contained at least six pages of A4 paper so they did what they always did and wrote three pages each and then added Tasha's one page of A4. They knew Tanya was having a rough time so they filled the letter with love, hope and positive thoughts. Of course everything was exaggerated. After all, this was a letter produced by three women who had grown up in the smudge. They had even included some 'YOU GET ME'S' and 'SWEAR DOWN'S' just to make her feel normal but also to project to the inmates that on the outside, they were 'ARD.

Joanne left after completing her version of exaggerated events on paper and now she was in her own moment, thanks to the incense she had brought from the shop built out of books and crystals, which had danced up her nose from the moment she had lit it. She was again in her own moment and it was being in her own moment she started the conversation of change with her daughter. Together they walked through 'The Magic land of Past' and shaped pathways to the future, whilst using their photo books as a form of exchange. It was in the form of you tell me yours and I'll tell you mine, where emotions led to the place of 'nothing I do is not good enough' and where The Shadow Self, Desire and Trigger held her hand whilst she used the ABC formula to show her daughter how they had ended up there.

It was the discussion of changes that had triggered her autobiographic memory into action, so much so she wanted to reflect on all the changes that had taken place over the years because she wanted to know the truth. It was the truth as to whether her addiction into finding the endless definition of self had really been a problem, as her daughter had described. But more importantly she now wanted to know if when she looked in the mirror, was she was actually seeing a true definition of self or was she was actually seeing others definitions of her.

Over the past few years there had been so much change. Everything had changed, including the history of smudge and those in it and she was going to go through the changes, even if it took her into the night. The past few years saw her redefine herself more than three times whilst chasing the endless definition of self in the psychological institution known as work. A friend she had grown up with and who she loved dearly had committed suicide and she hadn't known until the word 'suicide' flowed through the mouths of others.

Tasha had been sleeping with her sister's boyfriend and she didn't see it. Tanya was part of a notorious gang and she never questioned it. Venn had his life taken and she just made it to his funeral in time. Her uncle had died of kidney failure and she forgot to tell him she loved him. She had not spoken to certain friends in years and now one of them had moved to Australia. Her daughter had grown up and was now answering back. Recently she had walked past someone she knew, who was shooting up in the ally way and now they were dead. The list of changes went on through to the early hours of the morning.

After going through the changes she felt sad and angry at herself more than anything else because whilst serious changes where happening in other areas of her life, her addiction had blinded her from some and bound her to others. She knew she was never going to get that time back with those who had died or another time to help those in crisis. She questioned the small possibility that her support could have made a difference but she knew that there would never be another chance to watch her daughter grow up. It had all been in the name of the definition of self, to prove she had earned a respectful place in the world, the same thing that thousands of people are doing everyday to prove they are defined and successful.

She lived in a world determined to programme the mind into believing that definition led to success and was crucial to your existence, yet it took you away from the things you may never see again. For those whose pathways had not led them to search for answers or the definition of self, they could not prove they had earned a respectable place in the world which is why the world did not recognise them. "This is not what I want" she said, whist staring at her reflection that was now staring back at her in the bathroom mirror.

It was 1am in the morning and she had tears flowing down her face because she had regrets which were now pouring out from the tear ducts of her eyes. It felt as if her heart was leaking water. Her regret was not finding the time to spend time with Venn, her music guru who made her laugh and spent so much time giving her mixed tapes and CD's, so together they could start with the two step and end in a shake down. Her regret was not making the trip to Birmingham when she had first heard her uncle was ill, so she could tell him she loved him and thank him for being an amazing uncle. Her regret was not taking more time to watch her daughter grow up because she thought her daughter deserved to live in a material world like every other child. She regretted not walking down the alley way to take the hand of an old friend and put her on the pathway to hope. Her regrets flowed and placed themselves on top of other regrets. She cried.

Accepting the Truth

The reality was that she lived in a world where everything was defined and where everyone believed in the worlds mission statement; that being defined gave you some form of internal happiness and success gave you a better quality of life. It does if life is about material things; things that you can project you have earned a respectable place in the world. However her experience of world definition had not given her internal happiness. If anything it brought her nothing but pain and had often led her emotions to visit the place of 'nothing I do is good enough'.

She knew she had to work because not working was a struggle and life was hard enough. It was working that gave her independence and the confidence to deal with life. It gave her the means to explore the world but more importantly it stopped her from walking the pathways to boredom, which would inevitably lead to depression. In no way was it a True definition because her addiction to being defined did not put her on the pathway to the True Definition of self. Instead it sent her on the pathway to nowhere.

The Soul Exchange

Accepting the truth is hard for anyone, especially when you look in the mirror and believe what is looking back at you is a true reflection of self and a true reflection of what we wanted to see when we looked in the mirror. What if we don't like what is staring back at us at some point in our life? This was the reason why she could not make a connection with her own reflection in the bathroom mirror whilst staring at it and why she was now questioning who she really was.

All she saw in the mirror was an external face and she knew it was an external reflection because even though it did what she did, she didn't feel it. Her reflection did not project that it had feelings or convince her that it felt what she was now feeling and she knew why that was. It was because her reflection that was now staring back at her was a day behind.

Now looking at her reflection of yesterday, it made sense as to why her and her reflection were no longer connecting in the mirror. She felt a flutter of a vibration, the same vibration that she had felt in the shop built from books and crystals. She stood looking into the mirror asking her reflection if it had felt it too. There was no response from her reflection and she smiled because that was a test to prove, that the person staring back at her was not her, it was who she was yesterday.

She stood for five minutes embracing herself from yesterday as a form of respect that it had gotten her this far, but she knew from the moment she turned away from the mirror she would not see the reflection of yesterday again. She took one last look and in sync they smiled and her attention quickly turned to the fluttering vibration. Whilst trying to get to know this vibration during her moment, the vibration was fading and fading too fast for her to hold on to it .She thought that maybe her fear of the unknown had scared it away so she dried her eyes, looked in the mirror and said hello to her new reflection.

CHAPTER 17

Recognising Your Peak-Ness

Sitting on her bed at 1.30 am in the morning, she recalled all the times when she had been at her peak. She thought how funny it was when you referred to a time when you were at your peak. Clearly it changed with age and she remembered that once, being at your peak was all about impulsive behaviour and not giving a shit. Now she was calling other times in her life peak times too. 'The Magic Land of Alice' was also a time when she was at her peak because; she thought it was peak to have such an imagination that enabled her to travel pathways to her dreams.

Peak was now also having the ability to understand how 'The Magic Land of Past' worked and being able to manipulate it. Peak was being able to jump into the souls of young people to teach them the ways of a warrior because they too were confused and fighting their way through the defining process. Peak was the ability to go on a few speed dates and find new friendships that existed within, in order to gain a better understanding of attraction. Peak is learning your ABC's to suss how you may have ended up there. Peak was having the experiences that led to the questioning of everything but more importantly she believed that it was peak, that her body was able to give life and even though her addiction had caused her to lose her way, she thought it was peak that she had recognised it.

Now she wanted to find where internal happiness lived and she knew where she wanted to start looking and that was within herself. She understood that she had got it all wrong and that being defined in a particular way did not last long because as the experiences changed so did she. Often "I'm not the same person I was five years ago" flows through the minds of those who either, desire to return to a time in their life when they were at their peak or for those whose peak was a time best forgotten, the "I'm not who I was five years ago" was evidence that they too had been searching for something to prove they had earned a respectful place in the world.

She knew that as long as she had a job and could project she had earned a respectful place in the world, she would be defined endlessly. This was thanks to people's perceptions (that are known to live forever) and the list of numerous jobs that went on forever. All you had to do was continue to play another version of the Definition game.

1.45 am and she was still sitting on the bed questioning. What would my head stone say about me? , thinking of all the people she had lost. Where does internal happiness live, thinking that definition had not brought her internal happiness' and how will I know when I am there? Questioning where she was meant to be.

What is happy ever after? And why were those who had earned a respectful place in the world so unhappy? "Why did I do the things I did?" she thought, questioning her old reflection and why do I do the things I do, thinking of what shaped her behaviour. Why do people desire Love? Thinking it seems to be what everyone is looking for. What is this talk about Truth and why do people want it so much? Thinking of the quotes that flowed from the lips of thousands of people in search of it and her final thought was where internal happiness lived.

Her mind then re-wound itself to the days of 'The Magic Land of Alice' and one day in particular. It was the day when 'The Magic Land of Alice' had morphed itself into the pathways to reality, where signs no longer said carry on, instead they told you to, stop and you could witness yourself in the making. Well there she was, sitting on her bed at 1.45 am in the morning, reliving the pathways of reality and witnessing herself in the making. She joined all the A, B and C's together like the spaghetti junction.

It was her search for the definition of self that had led to wanting to find the endless definition and had given birth to an addiction, which had led to finding the shop built from books and crystals. That had led to finding out the truth about that word definition and it was the truth that had left her still questioning. The experience had given her the skills to recognise change, which motivated her to want to go through the changes. It was going through the changes that led to her question her reflection and that welcomed the soul exchange. This was the reason she was sitting on her bed, embracing herself and watching herself in the making. She invited the new vibration and it stayed around long enough for her to on to hold it. And it was holding it that led to a new vibration being born and its name was 'The Heart of the Tiger'.

The Ultimate Climax

'The Heart of the Tiger' was so powerful and unique she actually believed she had given birth to it. She believed that it had been there all along but for it to venture to the birth canal; she had to desire it with a great passion. Desiring it was like making love to yourself with all the climaxes that happened during previous climaxes. It would be the ultimate climax that would shift your mind, body and soul into the correct position, with all aspects of your existence forming a planetary alignment, where all three celestial bodies (the mind, body and soul) would generate a powerful vibration that only you can create.

This type of power is the ultimate peak because it could take years to give birth to something of this calibre and depending on which pathways you chose to walk, depended on if you ever give birth to it at all.

'The Heart of the Tiger' experience was going to take her on a totally different journey, one where the worlds definition did not exist and the pathways did not lead to 'The Magic land of Alice' or 'The Land of Past'.

The pathway of alignment was the answer to who she really was and now sitting on her bed with the powerful vibration for company and the world's definition disappearing along with her addiction, she no longer needed to prove she had earned a respectful place in the world, because it was this she was now questioning.

CHAPTER 18

The Truth

Pulling out a book she had bought from the shop built from books and crystals, curiosity's eyes were wide open and his feet were firmly on the ground. His energy was somewhat impulsive and impatient and he was eager to start the pathway of alignment. 'The Heart of the Tiger' on the other hand was still and patient but his presence was strong and open. Open to indulge and stand before what could come from walking the pathway of alignment.

'The Heart of the Tiger' and her curiosity had developed a playful relationship. It was one you would expect in the wild with two animals trying to prove whose heart pumped the hardest, to determine which one of them was going to lead the way. She was interested to see who would end up winning the play fight because she thought they both were powerful in different ways and played well together. However, even though she did think they were both powerful, she had secretly defined 'The Heart of the Tiger' as being the strongest and that was because her curiosity had insisted on finding out what his name actually meant. Curiosity claimed it was no fun play fighting with someone whose name was unknown. Curiosity being curiosity wanted to know who he was play fighting with, its temperaments, character, limitations and the dangers of playing with something of this calibre. It was here, 'The Heart of the Tiger' got its name.

The name that belonged to this new vibration was the SOUL keeper. She was not surprised; she believed that unexplainable experiences had shown her soul to her on many occasions and when she and her curiosity investigated further it made sense. She now believed all her previous life experiences, pathways and all her questioning, along with being able to join her A, B and Cs to understand how she had ended up there, were all a part of the process and led her to where she was meant to be, in the company of 'The Heart of the Tiger'

The Pathway of Alignment

Her new reflection that took shape from the soul exchange experience wanted to know the truth, the truth about who she was. She now desired nothing but the truth and that included having all the trues. (True love, True friendship, Her Truth, His Truth and THE TRUTH). Most important among the Truths was a True sense of self. (A true definition) She wanted this most because she believed this is where internal happiness would live.

Start with your name. This is what she thought, whilst sitting at her desk in the psychological institution defined as work. Her mother had told her once that she was going to be called Natalie. Natalie was the name that she had, on some occasions repeated back to herself whilst looking in the mirror. She actually questioned what the hell her mother was thinking. She praised the fact that the name Natalie had not flown from the ink, for it to dance around on the birth certificate. She often questioned who she would have been if she had been called Natalie and questioned as to whether she would have lived the same experiences, gone through the same pain and walked the same pathways. She also thought that it was strange how people's names seemed to suit them and that Tasha, Joanne and Tanya seemed to have been given the right name. So was the naming process intentional and not a coincidence?

Whilst opening the book from the shop built out of books and crystals, three weeks after 'The Heart of the Tiger' had travelled down the birth canal, it was "What's in a Name" that had her curiosity peering over her shoulder to get a glimpse of the gold book and its black ink that lived between the sheets. As before, the words were scrolling down her eyeballs whilst her free will was entering a world she was unfamiliar with.

The little gold book was a formula of how to use the black ink that lived in between the sheets to find the true meaning of a name and whilst reading, the black ink explained how numerologists who were real scientists, were clever enough to use numbers to foresee the pathways in which someone with that particular name would take. "Impossible." she said, scoffing a sandwich on her lunch break.

Her motivation for wanting to know the meaning of her name had originally stemmed from her curiosity's questioning regarding the name of her new vibration. It was also because of that, she believed if she was going to know who she really was, it was in the name she had been given. This was thanks to another book she had read looking for answers.

She followed the ink of the gold book and her curiosity vibration was becoming stronger, eager and somewhat impulsive to reach the destination of the naming process. It was 'The Heart of the Tiger' who told him to slow down because rushing only creates room for mistakes. The perfect one it said, after using the formula to dissect numbers that followed a detailed description of what defines someone with this name, however it also gave other definitions of the same name and its definition changed according to who was doing the defining. The little gold book was a book full of definitions. Palm tree and warrior were amongst the endless definitions and she felt her curiosity weaken because she was now facing another form of verbal diarrhoea. However, 'The Heart of the Tiger' stood firm with his foot firmly on the pathway of alignment.

Pissed off and somewhat disappointed that her curiosity's desire of doing, meant that he did not understand that everything in the world has its limitations and that it was his doing that had taken them on the pathway to verbal diarrhoea. It was a total waste of time and was the reason she was now questioning if anyone had the answers. She was now having an internal slanging match with her curiosity that included a lot of for fuck sakes. It is that thing that we do when we allow our curiosity to control us until we follow it to a dead end. Only then do we want to punch its lights out because we have not yet learnt that curiosity killed the cat. This had her feeling disheartened because the gold book claiming to have the answers did not.

Getting answers from the gold book is where she believed she needed to start. It would be the famous quote that everyone's talks about when they are lost. The "Having to start somewhere" is what she believed would open the gateway to the pathway of alignment. Because she did not know what her name meant, she felt she had failed. The word failure had played a major role in her life. She believed she had failed at relationships, being a good daughter, a mother, a colleague, a friend and in many cases she believed she had failed herself. Failing had often led her emotions to the place of 'nothing I do is good enough'.

After arriving home from work and having failure for company, she was restless. The gold book and its black ink that lived between the sheets had left her questioning why we even believe that books can give us the answers. After all, they are all based on someone else's interpretation of what is. Throwing her work bag on the floor the little gold book popped its head out as if to deliberately irritate her even more. It clearly did not know that irritating someone who had grown up in the smudge could be potentially dangerous.

She took one look at the little gold book and smiled. She then went to the kitchen and began furiously ripping out the pages of the gold book because her curious was now her delirious. As each page hit the floor, she defined it as being no better than her book of predators. They were both full of shit. Now looking at the black ink that no longer lived between the sheets but were now squatting on the floor, she put her hands in her hair whilst pulling it very tightly and wrapped it around her knuckles. She screamed. She wondered whether her psychological state of mind was now truly a place for the care of persons who are destitute, disabled or mentally ill. Her frustration was leading to the pathway of emotional distress just as the definition had predicted of someone born in October. (She was someone who was likely to become anxious and edgy when unplanned delays created uneasiness on the mind) and her frustration had given birth to her aggression.

Looking at the torn out pages on the floor, her OCD vibration was now intertwined with her frustration. She took a deep breath and picked up the homeless pages from the floor and with a simple "Oh well" she flung them in the bin. "I give up". She walked to the living room ready to send 100 watts of music through her soul, because it was going to be the 100 watts that she was going to use to send the feeling of failure into oblivion.

She started with the two step and on the verge of a shake down. She questioned if she was having some form of a breakdown, not even the 100 watts could not stop her from questioning why was it after you walked the pathways of world definition to prove you have earned a respectful place in the world, something supernatural or unexplainable within strived for you to do better, know better and be better?. It was possible that this new vibration, 'The Heart of the Tiger', was her new dictator.

Questioning her new dictator because of his strong presence, she had the feeling that he would not allow her to stop questioning. Why don't we just stop searching! She shouted into the room but her voice could not be heard because she had chosen to use the 100 watts to try and send her feelings of failure into oblivion.

'Knowing who you truly are will shape the pathways to true everything' is what she heard. She could not work out if what she heard had somehow found its way through the sound waves of the track that was playing. (Although the song was not being played backwards) she knew what she had heard.

'You are a warrior and you now believe that internal happiness exists in finding the True sense of self. Your inspiration has come from within because you want to continue your journey in life with love and understanding of self but to achieve this you must learn to understand what truly defines you as a person'. There it is again. 'Only then will you be peak enough to teach others who are struggling to find themselves in the world of definition and only then will you be peak enough to show them what True love , True friendship and what being True to yourself looks like'.

'Books and others knowledge can only give you ways to try, however books are still a version of someone else's definition and being true to yourself does not lie in the answers projected by others definition of what is the truth. It lies within the internal caves that exist within you.'

She put her hands over her ears and growled, "I just wish whoever is talking would just shut up," she said, not realising that it was actually her that was sending this message through the part of her brain that she had trained to deliver effective affirmation strategies, should she get stuck on the pathway of sabotage.

CHAPTER 19

Knowing When to Surrender

No matter how hard she tried to drown out the thoughts and affirmations that were now giving her a headache because they were in conflict with each other. The 100 watt vibration was now becoming over bearing and she craved silence. With failure for company and failing to send it into oblivion, she turned off the music and sat on the sofa in the Lotus position.

In the silence she could feel the feeling of failure and her affirmation vibration fighting the battle of the testosterone level. Now confused and questioning who was right and who was wrong, confusion created a force of negative energy that was floating around her emotional matrix and causing her to have the urge to surrender.

She always believed that she had spent most of her life fighting. If she was not fighting to define herself enough to prove she had earned a respectful place in the world, she was fighting with herself whilst walking the pathway of sabotage. She had always been her worst enemy and her previous experiences had seen her sabotage everything she desired because she believed that she did not deserve it. It was conflict with self that had always been at the root of her ability to sabotage; one minute thinking she will work towards it and when she had got it, it was the believing that she didn't deserve it which motivated her to tear it down.

Growing up in the smudge with limited everything, living with the labels she had not even written and having 'The Shadow Self' for an enemy had led her to believe in others definition of her and it was this that often put her onto the pathway of sabotage. Not only would she sabotage opportunities she would also sabotage herself, if someone told her she was beautiful her interpretation of that, was that she was ugly. If she was told she was smart, her psychological institution's interpretation of that was that she was thick. If someone told her she looked good, then she looked shit. Thin was fat and where she could succeed would be where she had failed.

If there was an opportunity that she could do, it was the 'can't do' that deliberately sabotaged it. She had always accepted someone else's definition of her and that included when a man told her he liked her, she was told to interpret that as he just wanted a quick fuck. It was not until her experiences had crossed the paths of those who she now believed came into her life for a reason, that sabotage is something she did less and less and thanks to a loving present given from a loving friend, affirmation was something she used, something she used to battle the sabotage demons.

It was during this time she had learnt when to surrender and knowing when to surrender meant surrendering the negative thoughts, feelings and other people's negative projections that you had allowed to walk through the doors of inner peace. You had to go to the place of surrender when you heard your soul cry. The place where it is believed hundreds of people go to surrender the feelings they don't like and or the thoughts from the words that planted limitation seeds, to prevent them from seeing what was really there. It was also the place where you surrender what you don't know and surrendering gave you the belief that it will come and one day you will know.

The Painful Shit

Having torn out the pages of the little gold book she questioned if she should surrender the feeling of failure because the negative energy was too painful. Confusion had caused her to want to hold on to it because she believed that's what women who grow up in the smudge do, hold on to painful shit because pain is what they know and it was pain that reassured them that they were alive. Only then do they know when they have suffered enough to want to let go because letting go of one thing made room for some other painful shit they felt they needed to hold on to.

Holding on to painful shit is typical of most. All women, especially those who grew up in the smudge held on to the painful shit. Those she had known who had been abused as a child had held on to the painful shit. Those women who had been hurt in the cave of love, held onto the painful shit. Those who were brought up in care, held onto the painful shit and those whose parents didn't give a shit about them, held on to the painful shit. She too was holding onto painful shit and was the real reason why she had spent half her life searching for the definition of self, to prove she had earned a respectful place in the world, because earning a respectful place in the world actually meant she did not have to face her painful shit.

She had seen what painful shit had done to those she had grown up with in the smudge and she too had seen what painful shit does to those who haven't. Regardless of where you were brought up she had concluded that all women hold on to pain like their life depended on it. She often questioned why women including herself held on to it, other than the assumption that it reminded you that you were alive and surely if there was a choice, women including her would choose to let it go as soon as the painful shit hit a nerve.

Now she found herself questioning why women would want to hold on to the painful shit. Her experience of painful shit had seen those holding on to it walk many different pathways to deal with it. Some pathways led to help me, some led to derangement, some had led to suicide and that included attempted and some led to the re- invention of self. Regardless of how many pathways she had seen people take their painful shit, she knew that painful shit had possessed the souls of many people including her. She knew she could never speak for or judge those for the pathways they had chosen to take their painful shit, but she knew should they choose to take their painful shit to her she would be there with her arms wide open. As for her holding on to the painful shit, it is what she did to prove to herself that she was strong enough to carry it and it was the testing of one's own strength that had led her to want to hold on to it, regardless of how painful.

She had not surrendered the feeling of failure yet because failure was going to be the one get out card she was going to use to project that finding a 'True sense of Self' would question everything , she called Joanne and asked her if she could get some weed (Cannabis). So that evening was spent with Joanne, reliving their peak experiences whilst laughing into oblivion.

The next day, with failure for company she went into the bathroom and sat on the toilet to do what she described as what all women should do every morning, to release yesterday's soul. Releasing yesterday's soul in the way of urinating meant that your soul was not riddled with yesterday's thoughts, people's opinions or all the crap that came with yesterday.

She felt rather limp and rough because she had forgotten what oblivion looked like. Well, up until she had chosen to let Joanne remind her, what smoking a £10 bag of weed (cannabis) can do to the brain. She smiled at the conversations that filled her living room the night before. Then her smile changed because now she was thinking of Tanya and it was thinking of Tanya that reminded her how she had not received a letter from Tanya in a while.

Still sitting on the toilet she questioned if Tanya could have done things differently, would she? She questioned if Tasha missed her sister and if she could have changed anything would she? And if she had an opportunity to really know who she was, would she? She kissed her teeth and rose from the toilet because regardless of her early morning questioning, she was late for work.

Her thoughts were going round and round in her head whilst she was on the bus on her way to work. Affirmation was still having a morning conflict with the feeling of failure and she was still questioning, would she? It was 'The Heart of the Tiger' who was now growling, sending shock waves through her system loud enough to stop affirmation and the feeling of failure in their tracks. 'The Heart of the Tiger's' words were now roaring in her ear for her to listen. The words were floating in large capital letters with exclamation marks attached to them telling her that she was deliberately walking the pathway of sabotage to prevent herself from ever finding the 'True Sense of Self'. And as much as she claimed that this was not the case, with aggression now having her back and still measuring her own strength in the way of the painful shit, it was the "I'm not ready" that started the thousands of excuses that were now flowing from her lips.

The Heart of the Tigers response to that was simple "You mean you're scared to let go of the painful shit?"

CHAPTER 20

Would You ?

It was the 'would you?' that had led her to wanting to know who she really was, but it was more to do with her curiosity, who had now been given permission to roam the grounds as long as he behaved. She knew that her curiosity and 'The Heart of the Tiger' had to get along because without either of them, the pathway of alignment could not be walked. She just needed to know how to tame them.

Her curiosity had the tendency to want to rush in and it was his rushing in that had often led to the 'for fuck sakes'. Regardless, she knew that her curiosity had the traits of a genius and without her curiosity she would have never questioned anything. Without her curiosity her mind would not have developed to its strongest point, where it was strong enough to warrior new adventures. If it had not been for her curiosity, she would have not been eager to learn and it was here she knew her curiosity wanted to learn, how deep, was the True Sense of Self.

The Heart of the Tiger was a new vibration and even though they had a long history it was not until she had given birth to it, did she actually remember it. His vibration was stronger than the rest and the rest were those who she had met from a simple speed date and because his vibration was so strong he was what she believed governed her soul.

Without 'The Heart of the Tiger', the relationships that exist within would not breathe or be strong enough to travel down the birth canal for her to meet them. Without 'The Heart of the Tiger' she would not possess the freedom of choice nor would she hold the divine essence of what others say defines her. Without 'The Heart of the Tiger' her journey would not have cultivated unique patterns of consciousness to deal with the challenges it experiences. But most importantly, without 'The Heart of the Tiger' she would not crave a life of internal happiness or the need to endlessly search to find it.

Craving had everything to do with her desire for a life where love was at the heart of everything and it was having true everything that she desired. She wanted to be at the heart of the understanding of self but more importantly, she wanted to be peak enough to understand and find the truth in others.

She wanted a life governed by the 'Soul Keeper' because she knew that he was the only one who was courageous enough to help her explore the truth and she believed that having a true sense of self was the beginning of having something to show to the world, rather than trying to earn a respectful place within it.

There Has to be More to Life

Arriving at the office, she sat at her desk with that ground hog day feeling and only the psychological institution defined as work for company. She turned on her computer and whilst she was waiting for it to do what it did every morning, she questioned if the computer could reboot itself differently would it? She even questioned if she got up from the desk and walked back out from where she came from, what would happen?

It was the loathing of routine that had led to deeper questioning and had her mind opening the doors to her other psychological institution, defined as the mind. "There has to be more to life" is what she was thinking whilst waiting for the computer to find a way to actually get itself together and upload. "There has to be more to life" the famous words she had heard so many times and it was "There has to be more to life" was a sign that she was vulnerable.

She had been vulnerable and seen vulnerable, even though she never really understood what vulnerable actually meant. Funny that, she thought with her head now in her hands, because for years she had worked in the community field where everyone was defined as being vulnerable. But what does vulnerable actually mean? Does it mean when you believe everything the world says or everything your man says? Does it mean you are not capable or is it for those who can't cope? Is it for those who have no trust or for those who trust too much? Does it mean you are not strong or is it for those who are weak? Does it apply to those who consider hurting themselves or to those who get hurt?

Is it for those who drink too much or for those who take drugs? Does it mean you are not aware or that you are gullible? Does it mean when you sleep around (because you're vulnerable to love) or is it for those like me who question everything? Or is it for those who spend their whole life searching?

She put her head in her hands as her mind had started the pathway to deeper questioning. It was the deeper questioning that made her vulnerable because now looking at the 'Who is Vulnerable' list, she recognised that she had been all of those at some point in her life and if this was a true definition of vulnerable, she concluded she had been vulnerable all her life.

Vulnerable led to questionable and she began to break down the word vulnerable in her head. Vul-ner-able. She dropped her bottom lip in confusion. What appeared was that unflattering forehead, causing her to squint, whilst running the word vulnerable through her head again. 'Vul-ner-able'.

Through her deeper questioning she was the one that now seemed to be in a bottomless pit, except in this pit you dig from the top down; unpacking and stripping back the layers of what the world of definition has taught you. Deeper questioning on this scale and thinking outside the box reinforced what she had already questioned. It was all so confusing.

On many occasions she had thought outside the box, more so when she was older. This was not because she wanted see the world in a different way or even question what she had been taught, but because thinking outside the box was forbidden, especially to those who were brought up in the Smudge. Those who dabbled in thinking outside the box were often defined as rebellious, defiant or as having major issues.

Thinking outside the box had led those who were peak enough to do it, to question everything. It would often send them onto pathways the world claimed to be forbidden (forbidden because knowledge is power) and was the reason why she believed that those small few that had been peak enough had ended up in history books. History books acted as inspiration. She had adopted the most inspiring "Well behaved women very rarely make history" and it was at the top of her number one list of one liner's. It was the "Well behaved women…" that she had often presented to those who defined her as rebellious, defiant or having major issues. She had used it as a statement to justify her behaviour, should she need to explain but it also meant that as she grew up she did it more and more. It was thinking outside the box that had questioned earning a respectful place in the world.

The 'Vul-ner-able' had her confused and made her question the language the world of definition uses to communicate. She looked out of the office window, glaring at the sunshine through the clouds. Who invented these words? Who decided on their definition? She wound her head back in from the clouds to watch her computer shine an electric blue, indicating it has just finished its morning coffee. The questioning of world communication continued. 'Why invent two words that actually sound the same but are defined differently'? she asked herself quietly. The computer pinged, taking her away from her deeper questioning and she sighed. Lucky for her she was saved by the computers ping because it was her boss who now had the glaring eye balls, beaming over in her direction, giving her the secret code for "get on with some work".

Knowing when Self Sacrifice Serves No Purpose

Now staring at the computer trying to reengage her mind, she sighed and that got the attention of Carrie-Ann. She kind of wished she had not sighed so loud because now Carrie-Ann's mouth was opening like a goldfish trying to pump oxygen into its gills. The girls, except the manager of course who was defined enough to have her own office, were now holding on to their breath and screwing up their faces because of the movement that was now happing in the room. That, of course, was the movement of Carrie-Ann's lips that had the girls in the room playing the eye ball game with each other, whilst sniggering and hiding behind their computers trying to look busy, should Carrie-Ann swivel her chair in their direction.

Everyone knew that once Carrie-Ann's mouth opened it was going to be open for at least the next twenty minutes because Carrie-Ann was defined as one of those girls that everyone found irritating. Not only was she irritating, she could talk forever. Carrie-Ann obviously was not aware of any full stops because Carrie-Ann had the tendency to jump over full stops like an athlete jumps over hurdles. "Are you ok?" started the marathon running from Carrie-Ann's mouth and it ran all on its own at a hundred miles an hour until she had reached the finish line. Even so, she always looked at Carrie-Ann whenever she spoke and always projected that she was listening, even though she had shut down her ears to the irritating thing she defined as Carrie-Ann Simpson's voice.

As she pretended to listen to the irritating voice of Carrie-Ann, her mind wondered and she was asking herself why she did it. Why did she have to go along with things just to make everyone else happy? Everyone does but why do we do it, she thought, looking into Carrie-Ann's eyes and smiling to project she was listening, all the while unpacking the words of communication that were coming out the mouth of Carrie-Ann Simpson.

Carry-Ann talked about how many days she had sighed that week, the reasons behind the sighs and gave a detailed list of all solutions relating to the sighs. The sighs were related to the PMT, sleep deprivation, the shit boyfriend, being bored of life, loneliness, a well needed holiday, feeling lost, being confused, fucked up friends and so on.

Staring into the eyeballs of Carrie-Ann sent her mind into overload because she was now running her own marathon in her head. She thought about where she was, where she is now and where she needed to be but more importantly her marathon had led her to the truth. The truth was, she was nowhere near finding the True Sense of Self because if she was she would not be listening to the irritating voice of Carrie-Ann Simpson.

She recalled how many times she had sacrificed her sanity for the happiness of others and took a deep internal sigh, attempting to look over the horizon. What she actually saw, was the horizon of Carrie-Ann Simpson's hair line and lucky for her, the world has the tendency to look at the line where the world seems to stop. In the case of Carrie-Ann's hair line, it was low enough for Carrie-Ann not to notice the eyeball shift.

Bored listening to Carrie-Ann, she began staring at the magnolia wall and with one finger in her mouth, biting at her nail that lived at the end of it. She drifted into the harmonious colour of paint that was splattered on the wall behind the head of Carrie-Ann Simpson, wondering about the internal caves, which had been described by 'The Heart of the Tiger' as the place to be explored to find the True Sense of self.

Having a great imagination and in the fuzz of Carrie-Ann's voice, she stopped unpacking the words of communication because the English language did not make sense. She drew an outline of her body which she referred to as the soul onto the harmonious horizon and used the power of her mind to create a piece of art on the wall. She continued to draw away, using only her mind and once she had finished she thought her art work was a replica of Vans Gough's sunflower painting; messy but it made sense to the eye. Fine lines led to the internal caves and displayed the route that must be taken to successfully walk the pathways that led to the True Sense of Self.

Studying her mess she had created from frantically drawing, she laughed because she thought it was funny that her biology lessons at school never mentioned caves, only tissues, muscles and bones. Is what she recalls. Then again she did question whether she had been in the toilet recruiting people for the fight against clone-ism over a cigarette when the lesson about internal caves happened.

Looking over the horizon and staring at her peace of art work and still biting her nails, she could see Carrie-Ann's mouth moving. She had not yet completed the thought process of what these caves were and how she was going to explore them. Neither had she questioned whether the fine art lines actually led to the caves, because the mess she had drawn was her interpretation of how to get there and not the mess of a professional cartographer whose interpretation would not be questioned.

Lacking confidence and questioning her own ability to find the True Sense of Self, she found Carrie-Ann staring her in the face looking rather irritated. "Are you listening?" were the words that shot out of Carrie-Ann's mouth, causing her to bring her eyes back from the horizon. The mess of internal caves disappeared and she placed her eyes back where they had started and that was in the eyes of Carrie-Ann, remembering that she was meant to be listening. Her words had failed to reach the part of her brain that translates world communication and there was a delay in responding. With not enough time for her response to go through her thought process, the face that she was now staring at her gave the impression that it was waiting for a quick response.

The mouth decease got the better of her and it was the simple "No," that had her smiling in the face of the marathon runner and what followed was the "You talk too much".

What Freedom Should Taste Like

After arriving home, smirking that she had finally told Carrie-Ann the truth, that she wished she had been brave enough to speak a long time ago, she questioned why it had been that day she had chosen to speak the truth and tell Carrie-Ann she talked too much. Even though Carrie-Ann looked upset by her statement, the truth hurts and they both had benefited from it. Carrie-Ann was given the opportunity to question it and she gave herself a taste of freedom.

She could have chosen to continue what she had been doing for years, listening to the irritating voice of Carrie-Ann Simpson and all the other things that led to sacrificing herself and her sanity for only others to benefit. What she was now calling a sacrifice of one's own happiness, to feed the ego-happiness of someone else, (thinking outside the box and evaluating the 'Carrie-Ann experience') proved sacrifice was not just about behaving or doing something that you did not want to do. Thanks to Carrie-Ann, sacrifice now included sacrificing your brain space for someone who, given a chance would off load their verbal Diarrhoea and cement it your brain cells just to feed their own ego happiness.

Throwing her work bag on the floor, the floor belonging to her living room internal thinking processes were happening in all directions, causing her to question why our brains could not stick to one subject. Her brain had the tendency to think and skip. Her brain had always functioned in this way and in this case it ended with the irritating voice of Carrie-Ann Simpson. It had started with the search for the Definition of Self, flown over the Magic Lands that led to the giving birth and ended with the True Sense of self, all in ten seconds.

During the think and skip that was now happening in the kitchen she turned the kettle on. Her think and skip had taken her from the

True Sense of Self to her previous thoughts about sacrifice and during this thought, the skip happened again. It took her to her earlier memories of sacrifice, confirming that sacrifice was something she had been taught. Her early memory of sacrifice was giving the toy that someone else wanted to them to make them happy because they would cry until they got it.

She then started thinking about all the other sacrifices she had made; following pathways to prove she had earned a respectful place in the world, sacrificing her role as a mother and denying herself of happiness because someone else wanted it. Putting herself on hold to deal with the drama that was making someone else unhappy and generally living a life where others happiness was more important than her own. During these thoughts she concluded that it was the pathway into adulthood where sacrifice was at its peak because not sacrificing yourself for someone else's happiness was defined as an insult and defined you as 'selfish' by those who's happiness depended on whether you fed them sacrifice seed or not.

It is the "Think of someone else for change "and the "Don't do it for you, do it for them" that often flows from the lips of thousands of people, including those who had spent a considerable amount of time on her pathway. Family, friends, lover's, bosses and colleagues were amongst those who believed that sacrificing your own happiness defined you as someone special. Bullshit.(now dabbling outside the box) Then whose life am I living? Sacrifice was just another institution; the institution of the soul is what she called it.

(Reflection led to deliberation and it was her conclusion that found the taste of freedom and gave birth to the firework vibration).

Staring into the coffee cup, watching the milk and the coffee granules dance the waltz, it was the reasons "why we did it" she believed were at the root of other peoples happiness. It had nothing to do with free will, but had everything to do with what the world of definition had led her to believe. She added hot water to her coffee cup and joined her A, B and C's together like the spaghetti junction. It was the failure of the gold book that led to having failure for company and also led to recognising the painful shit and knowing when to surrender.

It was the "would you?" that led to the willingness to walk the pathway to deeper questioning and the questioning of who she really was. It was the questioning of whom she was that led to the internal caves. She had seen these caves in the horizon and that led to finally understanding what freedom should taste like. It was the taste of freedom that recognised the sacrifices, empowering her determination and motivating her to dabble outside the box. Dabbling outside the box had led her to Reflection and Deliberation and it was her conclusion that introduced the firework vibration.

This new vibration was a sign she was ready to walk the pathway of alignment in search of the True Sense of Self.

CHAPTER 21

The Secret Ingredient

Having the ability to join her A, B and C's is what she used to understand how she had ended up there. If she had fucked up as least she knew why. If she felt confused, she knew that her ABC's would un-confuse her but more importantly it was her ABC's that would show her how she had contributed to the situation. Whether it was the choices she made or the things she had allowed to steer her choices. This had everything to do with the pathway to deeper questioning that led to the knowledge of all the possible reasons why pathways were created. In this case she believed her previous pathways were created to teach her how to master the ABC formula and bring her to where she was meant to be.

Regardless of what truth shaped the pathways, she understood that she may never really know. It was her belief that these pathways had been responsible for her becoming a Master of her ABC's and that inspired her to want to become a Master of herself. It was too easy to project what she wanted people to see, using the world's interpretation of definition, to prove she had earned a respectful place in the world. . Doing so was painful to the soul.

Painful to the soul means rubbing out your true colours to match the damp colourless souls who were willing to sacrifice themselves in order to blend in. Eliminating the bright vibrant colours that truly defined them because they had never questioned the world of definition and are happy to survive in the grey Smudge coming up for air whenever they could, not yet recognising this is not where internal happiness lived.

(The real challenge that would measure her strength would be to get out the paint brush and dance in vibrant colours, painting the air and making vibrant footprints as she walked the pathway to the unknown, projecting her middle finger to the world of definition as she went).

Her curiosity vibration was present and roaming the grounds with his eyes wide open and it was her thoughts of being peak enough to become a Master of herself that had her curiosity excited. She believed that being a master of herself would be the most powerful gift she could give to herself and would warrior the rights of her soul rather than, allow others to poison it with their limitation seeds and biased knowledge of what is. It was 'The Heart of the Tiger' that was now telling her in order to become a Master of self. She must explore the caves and tame her curiosity. Not all caves were easy to travel nor were they all pleasant. "Pleasant or not they belong to you," is what he was claiming. "They are the rare ingredients that truly define you. Only then will you know if this is where internal happiness lives along with the hidden formula to having true everything".

His statement got her excited not because she was actually taking in what he was saying; somewhere inside her is where 'something to prove' lived. She called it her 'anal side' because every time she had been told that she couldn't do or that places were potentially dangerous, dark or worse and she could come out of it worse than she went in, it was often these words that fed her alter ego and it was the alter ego that had something to prove regardless of the consequences.

Many times she had gone in, guns blazing with her curiosity also having, his own set of guns engraved with his initials; both acting like tomb- raiders that had not carried out a proper risk assessment and on almost every occasion, she had been affected.

Sitting on the sofa with that something to prove feeling the phone rang. It was Tasha (Miss Hotness to the Universe and to all men). There was no hello. Instead she was greeted with "I've fucked up" and when she asked Tasha what she meant it was the "I'm pregnant" that shot out of the phone speaker. "What is wrong with you!" she said whilst kissing her teeth and thinking Tasha needed the ABC formula.

Tasha explained that a new guy she had met had been injecting another form of internal happiness inside her for months and on many occasions he had pulled out, but on the last occasion, he had said that her pussy was so good he could not help himself. There was a five second silence in between Tasha speaking her final word and it was the response of her mouth disease that could not help itself; "Well your pussy's failed you now". She had used a remixed version of Missy Elliot's track "Pussy don't fail me now", a cherished classic from her R&B collection being the appropriate response that she felt Tasha needed to hear.

Listening to Tasha's response (she was shaking her head) she questioned why it was, that some women projected the same behaviour patterns over and over again even though their previous pathways had shown them the same outcome more than once. She questioned why some women avoid condoms like the plaque and then want to freak that they had caught a sexually transmitted infection again, or in Tasha's case got pregnant again. Tasha was still talking, so it was her first question that led to the deeper questioning regarding some women's behaviour.

She questioned why those who are addicted to love kept asking the same type of man to step onto their pathway just to act like clones of the ones before them? Why women see the signs that they have seen before but choose to believe that the same signs don't mean what they meant the last time? Why those who desire to chat about others people's business, continue to do so, when they are fully aware of what chatting about people's business can do, from previously walking the 'chatting about people's business pathway'. But why was Tasha's even thinking of having another baby, when her previous pathways had led to all her children being fatherless?

"No this one is different! He is good with the kids and he said he will be there" said Tasha. This brought her out of her internal questioning about some women's behaviour. It was at this point she laughed to herself because she recalled two occasions where Tasha had used the exact same statement and it was the same statement used to justify her two previous pregnancies. Have women not yet learnt that having the same behaviour patterns can only ever produce the same or similar outcomes. Hence, the worlds definition (history repeating itself).

Tasha's voice and statements had her questioning Tasha's behaviour. Did Tasha's behaviour patterns have something to do with her past or her insecurities? Is it that Tasha allowed men to plant limitation seeds to prevent her from becoming anything other than what she was, a woman who had an addition to men or was it that Tasha knew nothing else but crazy? The definition of crazy in Tasha's case was following the same pathways in hope of a different outcome, regardless of why, she concluded that in Tasha's case it was evident Tasha was in search of that thing called internal happiness and she believed that Tasha thought that somewhere in a man's soul is where internal happiness lived.

Despite her problems, Tasha was not questioning a termination and that had led her to believe it was the pathways that people travelled in search of internal happiness that had been at the root of some bad choices and depending on how badly you wanted to find it, depended on what you would do to get it. She believed that the definition of internal happiness depended on who's doing the defining. To some it is about revenge, to others it is living in denial, to him it's about money, to her it is about entrapment and to them it is about being in control. To most it is about searching for the true meaning of internal happiness, often looking elsewhere to find it but very rarely looking within themselves. After all, she had searched for internal happiness in many places and that included taking drugs, criminal activity and men. All had failed to reap the seed of long term internal happiness which is why she now recalled them as being bad choices.

Tasha had talked her last sentence and in a long conversation about choices and how Tasha had contributed to the situation and allowed men to define her was a true picture of how Tasha had ended up there. Lovingly she gave Tasha the ABC formula as Tasha cried down the phone. She hoped that Tasha would use it in the same way she had because it beckoned upon crazy to walk your previous pathways like ground hog day in hope that the outcome would be different.

Now soothing Tasha's pain, which came from understanding that history was repeating itself, she told Tasha that once she had mastered the ABC formula, she would teach her how to manipulate it, because she believed that Tasha was someone who needed something that she could use to foresee her future pathways.

The secret ingredient to the ABC formula was its flexibility, the ingredient that helps to shape itself according to what you want it do. You can use it in its original form to understand how you ended up there or manipulate it to show where future choices would take you, giving you the ability to predict the outcome of un-walked pathways. By giving this to Tasha, she believed she had shown something to the world.

CHAPTER 22

The Power of the Imagination

Now bored after a gruelling day at work and having to deal with the subliminal messages that were being projected from the eyes of Carrie-Ann and still having that something to prove feeling, her curiosity wanted to play. They had thought about nothing else for days and now they were curious. They wanted to know where they were, what they looked like and how they were going to get there. She questioned how she was meant to tame her curiosity that was now jumping around, showing his guns and demanding they go in search of the internal caves. However on this occasion she declined and gave him a full list of how listening to him in the past had often led to the 'for fuck sake's' whilst reminding him it was only ever her that had been affected.

Leaving her curiosity sulking somewhere in her matrix it was her imagination that now had her attention. Her imagination had always saved her from the place of boredom. She often imagined her wedding day as she was growing up and how her parents were going to surprise her with that BMW for passing her exams. She often questioned what happened to her imagination as she got older. She blamed puberty for the sudden change. She no longer imagined her virgin wedding day because she was no longer a virgin nor the perfect surprise because it never came; instead her imagination had become somewhat impulsive and in some cases took her to places she would not dream of talking about. Sometimes it would be the sleeping with her cousin when the sex with the one night stand was boring or sometimes lying naked in a pile of fifty pound notes. The imagination, which linked to her fantasies, saw three gorgeous men and three dark skinned women stroking her with a feather as she lay in a canoe smiling in the Garden of Eden.

Her imagination had the ability to take her anywhere and she had always had fun with it because she often used her imagination to foresee a response to, if her baby father could see her now. It was often what her knight in shining armour would look like and how he was going to cut down trees and fight fierce dragons to save her that captured her imagination. She had always had this feeling of wanting to be saved but never really knew what she needed to be saved from, other than the downfalls of life. (This was when life was the one who wanted to test her strength by throwing its life sucking darts at her whenever it felt like it).

She knew that there were occasions where she had no control over her imagination and she knew that because of some of the dark places that her imagination had taken her. It varied from brothels, to being blind folded, from pimping out bitches to violent acts of sexual domination and even calculating the perfect murder. A kidnapping that made front line news and chopping off his dick were included but it was always the perfect robbery that had her smiling.

She had questioned if all women had an imagination like hers, an imagination that changed as they got older, one that they could not control and one that dug into their deepest sexual fantasies or led them to the places that were forbidden. It was only ever the fifteen year old girl that she recalled, who had been openly honest during talks about sex and some of her sexual fantasies, had been defined as extreme. It was always Joanne who would openly admit that her imagination often involved the kidnapping and torture of Dan for fucking up her childhood.

She could not remember at what stage in her life her imagination had changed but she did know that people's imagination had the ability to take them anywhere. A hidden image formation that linked to the life experiences of an individual. She believed that the pathway into adult hood exposed her to many things, things that were defined as the norm for someone standing on the adulthood pathway. Aggressive sex, watching threesomes on the porn channel, a murder being projected on the TV screen and the 10'oclock news claiming it was the greatest bank robbery. The rage of going to the movies to watch the latest film that showed scenes of violence and also included the chopping off his dick with explicit sex scenes, sent subliminal messages that tapped into her darker side.

They all created an image formation that attached itself to her imagination whether she wanted it to or not. She had questioned if this was the reason that she had lost control of her imagination sometimes, causing her to visit the darkest of places that had her blind folded and pimping out bitches. Regardless of what had contributed to the change in her imagination, she still had some ability to steer it in the right direction.

Lighting a cigarette in the awe of her boredom, she held it between her two fingers like it was still deemed sexy to see a woman smoke. The cigarette she held at the window (between the caves of her fingers) had caused a trail of smoke as the cold air touched. In awe of her boredom she had the ability to suck the life out of it and create a puff of smoke that chugged in the air looking a lot like a cremation that was on its way to heaven.

She was staring out the window and thinking of Tanya and questioning everything that had to do with Tanya. How she was coping, why had she not got a letter and she even questioned if she got their letter. She imagined what it would be like to be a prisoner and even questioned if she could do it. Doing it had everything to do with being locked up with hundreds of bitches who had been locked up because they too were searching.

She questioned whether the rumours about prison were true because prison was something of an interest to her and it had started with her first visit a week after Tanya had been convicted. The more visiting orders she got and the more she went, the more it became of interest. She had always defined women in prison as your rough neck girls from the other end of the Smudge. They were the type of girls who you expected to go to prison. However, visiting Tanya made her question herself because she saw that women in prison were vulnerable.

Those who she defined as being vulnerable were those she had spoken to during her visits. For example, the mother of...... who was in prison for killing her husband in self-defence because she had a choice to kill or to be killed. There was a woman who was in prison for the abduction of her daughter because she had an addiction to crack cocaine. The ex boyfriend had got custardy, even though she had been clean for three years. Clearly, the missing had become too much. There was a girl who was addicted to love so much; she showed her true love by injecting what he had given her and the woman who turned to prostitution so her children did not have to grow up with limited everything. They all had the same thing in common. They too were searching. Some were searching for their definition of internal happiness and others were searching for a new definition.

It was only through experiencing prison, did she know vulnerable. Regardless of their act, she thought it was sad that she had defined them as rough necks, believing the hype and the stereotypes that the world of definition projects into the souls that have not yet questioned because they too are too busy searching. For those who sentences were justified, and that included Tanya, they too were vulnerable. She realised that she had been right all along in believing that those who did not earn a respectful place in the world were not recognised in the world. Because if they were recognised .... is where she ended.

Thanks to her imagination taking her on a virtual tour as an act to bring her away from her boredom, she realised that she could not do prison. She knew that she had to change the way in which she allowed her imagination to control aspects of her brain because even though the perfect robbery made her smile, her ability to use the ABC formula would steer her away from the un-walked pathway to nowhere.

Her thoughts did the think and skip from places that her imagination had taken her to and where her friend's imagination had taken them. It was her imagination that was now questionable.

Something To Prove

Having her imagination and something to prove for company, it was the place where something to prove lived that had her curiosity returning from the matrix showing his guns. She simply told him to put down his guns and calm himself because he would not need them. She had no idea how to tame her curiosity and she did not even know if she wanted to because if it had not been for her curiosity, she would have never embarked on the journey of deeper questioning. (In search of the 'True Sense of Self').

Finishing her cigarette and in awe of her boredom, her mind set on the internal caves. She knew that the caves had the answer and her curiosity still wanted to know how deep, was the 'True Sense of Self'. But it was 'something to prove' who was now irritating her because he was the one difficult vibration that had been around forever.

Many times she had tried to evict him from the place where he lived but unfortunately for her, he owned properties all over the place. Not only did he live in her but he lived in others. He was a gangster, employed to carry out the dirty work of the alter ego with his own firm of gangster wannabee's. He went around terrorising people into proving themselves and for those who were finding it hard or could not prove themselves; they were often confronted with the beating sticks that belonged to the firm.

All the associates at the firm of 'something to prove' had names that reflected the job that they had been given. Anger, he was the feisty one and his position within the firm was to generate fireballs into the souls who were finding it hard or failed to prove, terrorising them until they had learned to hate themselves. Disappointment, he was the one who dug the graves for those who had given up and Frustration prayed on the minds of the vulnerable, always telling them there was another way whilst leading them to the grave.

Tears had a soft side, showing his heart when he heard the souls cry and he was the one telling them they would be ok. However 'something to prove' had a brother and he too was in the firm but like most organised firms, there's always room for rivalry and it was Determination who would chant the forbidden words of the firm, telling souls to try or keep trying. (For the love of their soul) In return for their efforts he would be willing to pick up the limitation seeds, should they choose to go against the alter ego and work for him instead.

Going against her alter ego for her love of her soul, she wanted to prove she was ready. Even though she was fearful, remembering 'The Heart of the Tiger's' statement; that not all caves were pleasant. She knew that she had to know. She recognised where she had started and how the pathways had been shaped to get her this far and regardless of the truth that lied behind these pathways; she believed she had been given a mission.

She believed that all her previous experiences that had led to the questioning of everything, opened gateways to hidden pathways that allowed to her experience rare and extraordinary things that questioned life and its purpose. Building relationships that existed within, had travelled down the birth canal to teach her extraordinary things to broaden her horizons and remove the limitation seeds, sending herself in search of a True Definition.

It was the extraordinary knowledge that had led to enlightenment and the manipulation of a programmed mind. She had the ability to think outside the box in order to see things clearly now. She knew her pathways had led her here for a reason. This reason had given birth to the firework vibration that was somewhere in her matrix and she felt it.

(From tags of ownership of those who were lost to those who acted like clones. Those who were striving to earn a respectful place in the world to those with nothing. Those that had something to prove and for those who were willing to start somewhere. Those who had visited 'nothing I do is good enough' and for those who were asking why they did it. For those who were searching for the truth, just as for those who were asking where internal happiness lived. For those who were still searching and those who felt as if their thoughts were stuck in a lift. For those who were walking around with labels they had not even written, to those who were willing to sacrifice and for those whose imaginations had failed them) all of whom were the reason.

Her mission was to explore the darkest of caves to teach those who were asking if she knew the 'True Sense of Self', the formula. The formula she believed existed and contained the rare ingredients of someone's true identity. After all it is "Be True to your self" that she had heard a thousand times that flowed from the lips of many. She often questioned how it was possible if you have never questioned and lived in a world where others definition is paramount to your existence.

CHAPTER 23

The Caves

With her imagination having the ability to take her anywhere and curiosity roaming the grounds, it would be the words of her determination that created a playful playground, whilst sitting down on the sofa. Thanks to her imagination and her dysfunctional relationship with her curiosity. She was now playing in the playground of 'I wonder if'.

She often blamed boredom for the strange things she did. This included laughing at herself, by herself when thinking her imagination was taking the piss. She often questioned if others did it or was she the only one in the whole wide world that had too much fun with her imagination. After all it was her imagination that had introduced her to the imaginary friend and later that turned into the imaginary boyfriend. Her imagination had always had the tendency to be extreme and the more bored she was the more extreme her imagination became.

In the playground of 'I wonder if', her imagination was forming playful tunnels that she assumed led to the internal caves. She asked her imagination what it was doing. Her intention was for her imagination to take her away from her boredom to embark on a playful journey to the internal caves because she wanted to prove she could do it. Even though the caves were not real and just a figment of her imagination, it would be the playground of 'I wonder if' that would act as the training ground to prepare her for the real thing.

She questioned if she knew herself enough to steer her imagination in the right direction, regardless of how well she did or did not know herself her imagination could never get it right. Her imaginations extremism had always added weird or strange things to the environment it was creating, that she had always defined as very unrealistic but in this case she had hoped that her imagination would have provided her with a realistic training ground, given she was on a mission.

Her imagination had a mind of its own and now finding it hard to control her imagination, she questioned why there were two native Indians sitting around a wigwam humming and smoking on a bong, looking rather peaceful in the playground of 'I wonder if'. It was often her imaginations lack of ability to get it right sometimes that had her laughing to herself by herself and seeing the Indians with her internal eye, she believed that the image formation may have had something to do with the knowing. Knowing that the place where her imagination was taking her had a spiritual connection. However, that did not explain the yellow mushrooms with red dots or the man who was coming down the slide with goat hooves for feet or the little people carrying large bread crumbs in their satchels. She put it all down to her ability to remember her childhood memories where films, books and TV had created an image formation that were now somehow getting caught up within the environment of her imagination.

Deeply in awe of her imagination and using all that she knew from her previous life experiences, she was now adapting to the weird surroundings that existed in the playground of 'I wonder if'. Her imaginations extremism made her wonder if there was the cave of the Baby Mother... Now she was taking the piss.

Curiosity now very excitable led her through the playground and with her internal eye, she became excited. What a wonderful place she thought and it was her imagination that had created it. This was a place that was limitless. Nothing was impossible. Now, she had developed the power of speed and using her new power she zoomed around the playground embracing all the strange things because she wanted to see it.

Even though her imagination had given her the power of speed, pushing her in one direction and then the other, she sensed that time was of the essence. She wished she had the time to speak to the native Indians but she spun that thought back on its self. She didn't really want to speak to them per say, what she truly wanted was to have a puff on their bong because she was curious as to what they were smoking. She also wanted to ask the little people where they were taking their bread crumbs and ask the man with hooves for feet what it was like, but in fear of it all fading away, she knew she must carry out her mission. Her mission was to use the playground of' I wonder if' for the purpose it had been created and that was to prove to herself she was ready, ready to walk the pathway of alignment to find the True Sense of self.

Conscious of time, she was finding it hard to take this situation seriously. Although she was working really hard to steer her imagination in the right direction, in the direction of the internal caves, she could not resist the temptation. Now she was laughing to herself, by herself, whilst sitting on the sofa demanding that her imagination take her to the cave of the Baby Mother.

The Cave of the Baby Mother

The Cave of the Baby Mother was the place where those who have questions go on a regular basis. It was a cave full of baby mothers asking why. Why was it that since they had joined the baby motherhood, the name they had been given at birth meant nothing. It meant nothing because the new definition they had been given was that of the baby mother or depending on which definition you'd prefer (the mother) known to be the baby mother's ancestor.

She too had been defined as the baby mother from the first day she became an official member of the baby motherhood club at nineteen. She had heard only too often the words "your so-and-so's baby mother?" She did not mind at first. Being the first baby mother defined you as Elite (someone special) and someone who was to enjoy soaking up all his love and his undivided attention. Wrapping yourself in his arms feeling pregnant and safe with his hand running down your neck and landing itself on your breast, where he squeezed softly to prevent the breast milk from leaking.

The intense touch meant you could not wait for the day you was not pregnant so you could ravish him in the traditional Urban London style of true love making. Where your imagination could run wild, picking up all the limitation seeds so that no sex position was impossible because in your mind after nine months with no sex, (just in case his penis should touch the baby's head), it was going to be the best sex he ever had. That was until the memories of child birth had hit him, causing him to remember how far your vagina expanded and it was only then did she question why his touch was never the same.

It was only when the questioning of touch turned to the question as to why he never looked at her in the same way, did he leave. To then allow three other women to join the same baby motherhood club. It was only then that she began to look at the definition she had been given (the baby mother of Marcus Davis) as an embarrassment.

With her imagination now taking her deeper into the Cave of the Baby Mother she saw Tasha. Of course with Tasha having three children by two different men, she questioned if Tasha had ever visited the Cave of the Baby Mother and given that Tasha was still trying to grasp the concept of her ABC's, she doubted it. Regardless of this, she saw Tasha and those in a similar situation to Tasha with her internal eye, standing in the cave of the baby mother.

Some had different baby fathers and some had the same baby father, regardless of fathers they were all sitting by the lake that ran through the heart of the baby mother cave. Each with their bare feet resting in the water was asking themselves why. For those who had children with one man, they questioned why their definition kept changing. Most recalled that the birth of the first child had defined them as elite and in many cases a wife; this was a title that had been given to them by him to show his appreciation. But once the second child came along they believed their definition had changed from the wife to her indoors and should there be a third, thanks to his alter ego having something to prove, it was the breading machine that they believed defined them.

Even so there were those extreme women who had an extreme imagination that caused them to take their breading machine grievance to the Cave of the Baby Mother to ask why their womb had been downgraded. This had everything to do with being defined as to having too many children and for those who had too many children by different fathers, the world of definition had a list of other definitions, which the world would use to define them.

For those who could not have children, the Cave of the Baby Mother was a place for them to pray to be blessed with the experience of becoming a mother either through adoption or IVF. Being defined as not capable made them vulnerable and for those who found motherhood a challenge, the cave of the baby mother was where they visited many times to ask why they had children in the first place.

The Cave of the Baby Mother was also the place, thanks to her extreme imagination for those who shared the same baby father to have it out with all the other baby mothers. They were all fighting for their claim to fame, screaming and shouting at each other, all tapping into their emotional matrix looking for the definition they wanted in relation to one man. She stood watching with her internal eye, remembering all the times she went to the cave of the baby mother to do exactly the same thing. But, thanks to all her previous pathways and life experiences, she thought they should just accept, regardless of how beautiful they were, who was the first, who he said he loved or who he was still fucking, the truth was one was no more deserving than the other. All but one, had chosen to join the same baby motherhood club and had they questioned or had grasped their ABC's; many would have foreseen the future pathways that were attached to this one man.

She left the Cave of the Baby Mother and feared how much time she had left before her imagination would fade or before something would distract her. Her curiosity got out his guns as she wondered what was happening. The playground of 'I wonder if' became grey and airy. All the wonderful but strange things that were created were scattering way. She saw it with her internal eye. The little people were running away and then there was nothing.

It was darkness that now dominated the playground of 'I wonder if' and the lack of her ability to control her imagination had caused the slide to perish along with everything else. Her imagination had ventured into an internal cave.

She remembered that it was 'The Heart of the Tiger' that said that not all internal caves were pleasant but this was not the reason her imagination had taken her here. It was the place she had visited it many times before.

The Cave of Darkness

The Cave of Darkness, she assumed (because it was just a figment of her imagination) was the largest of all internal caves and so large it had two tunnels. One tunnel led to the unknown and although she had visited many times before she had been too scared to venture it. Even though, her curiosity had tempted her on many occasions. She knew where this tunnel could lead and she had seen those who had travelled down it come back because they were too scared to carry on. Some never came back. The second tunnel is where she had travelled before. It was the tunnel that her uncontrollable imagination had taken her to on many occasions and it would be where she kept her darkest fantasies. The place where pimping out bitches and the perfect bank robbery had left her smiling.

The two tunnels were the opposites of darkness and the entrance belonging to each faced each other. The tunnel on the left led to the unknown and those who had travelled down it and returned (too scared to carry on) had left sticky notes on the wall of the tunnel near the entrance, sharing their experience. The notes included why they had ventured the tunnel to the unknown and why they had come back. The sticky notes also gave the name of the traveller with detailed descriptions of what to expect from travelling this tunnel. Those who had returned defined themselves as weak because they had failed to walk into the unknown.

The tunnel on the right led to hidden fantasies that were waiting to be discovered. It was the tunnel where people would spend hours exploring and the further they ventured, the more captivating their fantasies became. For some, the deeper they went, the darker the fantasy. Many explored just for fun but for others it became an obsession that led to hours and hours of exploring and the deeper they ventured down it, the longer they explored and the more they explored the more dark and extreme their fantasies became. Both tunnels existed in the heart of the cave and when her imagination did not want to explore her deepest fantasies, it was the place that her imagination would take her when her soul was black.

She wanted a place where she could hide her deepest and darkest feelings of sadness. The place where she had hidden her glass bottle years ago lived in one of the small alcoves in the cave wall. This was the place she went to bottle it up. Only when that bottle was full would she know if her curiosity was powerful enough to make her curious enough to venture down the tunnel to the left that led to the unknown.

She cried. She remembered how her imagination had the ability to send her anywhere, from happy places to secret places; it was the place of the glass bottle she visited the most. It was the bottle that silenced her pain and every time she visited she could see all the things that had contributed to her sadness, old and new because she could see them through the glass.

Many times she promised herself that the next time she visited the Cave of Darkness, rather than add 'sadness' she would take one sad thing out of the bottle and address it, in hope that if she did this on a regular basis, one day the bottle would be empty. Her bottle was never empty. She had learned to use the bottle to measure her strength and she measured her strength according to the level of the painful shit that projected itself through the glass every time she visited. What started the crying as her imagination started to fade, bringing her out of the Cave of Darkness was, she had not kept the promise she had made to herself. And more she had questioned the tunnel on the left, contemplating suicide many times.

The environment of her living room started to regain its focus and she knew that she was no longer in the playground of' I wonder if' because her imagination had gone quiet. All that remained were the fading images belonging to the Cave of Darkness that were floating around her emotional matrix causing her soul to feel black. She remembered all the painful shit and commanded that her affirmations show themselves.

She used the experience to measure her strength and entered the Cave of Darkness one last time. She quickly put a lid on it and dried her eyes, leaving the Cave of Darkness behind.

It took four days for the residue belonging to the Cave of Darkness to disappear. During these four days she indulged in nothing but sadness. She knew putting a lid on it did not ease the pain; even so, it was the one thing she could do to keep her pain bottled up in one place. No one knew and so no one ever questioned the little glass bottle that she kept in one place. (The bottle that held her secrets of sadness)

The truth about the power of one's imagination is that it is "hidden". It is where image formations take place without the knowledge of others and depending how you measured your strength depended on how far you would go to pretend the Cave of Darkness did not exist. Friends and family would not question the depth of the cave and had they questioned, she believed those close to her would have known when she was depressed and that she had questioned the tunnel to the left.

CHAPTER 24

The Internal Caves

She received a letter from Tanya the day after the residue of the Cave of Darkness had disappeared. Tanya's letter made her smile because it was a letter that you would expect from someone who had grown up in the Smudge.

It included hand drawn smiles, paragraphs that were written in different coloured ink because it had been written over a four day period, where ink smudges blended with one another. The letter sent motions down her spine and whilst reading the pages she soaked up a range of Tanya's emotions. Words danced around on her majesty's paper to the sound of the national anthem. Tanya's words were formed in a way that asked how she had ended up there. Tanya's letter made her question if Tanya could have done things differently, would she? It also made her aware how prison had sent Tanya to the darkest of places and even though Tanya had followed the prison rules, nothing she did was good enough.

She read how many times Tanya had looked in the prison mirror and hated the person she had become, acting like a clone to hide her true colours in order to blend in. How the prison system had failed her because she tried to tell them she was vulnerable. How being locked up twenty hours a day had sent Tanya's imagination to the darkest of places and it was here Tanya had confessed that she had been curious to walk what was known as the tunnel to the left.

Reading the letter she became emotional because Tanya's letter had projected a mirror image of some of the places she had been. She wished that she could tell Tanya about her ABC formula but there was not enough time. As she read on, the letter contained all the promises that Tanya was making with herself; promises of hope and hoping to re-gain acceptance from others because Tanya knew that the pathway that had led to prison is what now defined her.

Tanya wrote how she was anxious that the world she had left would not recognise her but it was Tanya wanting to start somewhere that shone like a star, transforming the ink from blue to silver. Tanya was making a promise that one day she'd find herself because thanks to the experience of prison, she was walking around with the labels she had not even written.

Despite everything, the words at the end of Tanya's letter were sentences of hope. They were sentences of what freedom would taste like because it was here that she read Tanya was getting her freedom. Tanya was going to be released from her institution in six weeks time.

Tanya's letter was a weird form of inspiration she could not explain. But she could feel it. Little did she know, whilst reading Tanya's letter a magical thing was happening. Tanya's sentences of freedom had lit her firework vibration. She had always believed that inspiration existed in someone else's raw (real) situation but there was something else happening. It was so powerful she cried. She was not sure if they were tears of happiness because Tanya was coming home or something else.

Whilst reading Tanya's letter her three celestial bodies (the mind, body and soul) had connected and aligned themselves in the correct position, creating a connection wall that vibrated in harmony. This connection wall opened her soul in order for her to receive and now her soul was truly open for the first time in her life. There were no barriers protecting her from the truth and there was no desire to sabotage it. Here was the opportunity and she knew it. She knew it because she saw 'The Heart of the Tiger' (the soul keeper) once again, standing firm on the pathway of alignment that led to who she really was.

She heard the words of her determination; "do it for the love of your soul" and she knew that somehow she had tamed her curiosity because he was not eager to rush in. Anxious, she ran the ABC formula in her head to foresee where the pathway of alignment could lead and she smiled because she knew, regardless how good or bad it was, it was the truth about her.

She needed to know and she desired the truth. Being accustomed to a life where world definition had the power to programme your mind was killing her soul and had erased the vibrant colours that truly defined her.

CHAPTER 25

The Internal Caves (the secret ingredient)

She questioned how it was possible that Tanya's letter had caused her three celestial bodies to connect and open her soul like a galaxy. She defined the experience as a galaxy because it was the only definition she could use to explain it. Her soul was truly open and she knew it because there were no barriers. She could not see them or feel them and it was her strange willingness to receive without fear that overwhelmed her.

Standing on the pathway of alignment, holding the hand that belonged to 'The Heart of the Tiger', she asked him how this experience was possible. He simply told her that it was the inspiration that she saw in Tanya's letter. Inspiration was, one of the world's mysteries that had caused her mind body and soul to connect. He also claimed that she had been introduced to the mind, body and soul many times before (via the use of her imagination, her emotions and her heart).

They had been the very things that had been active during her lifetime but she had never made the connection. Looking confused, she asked him to explain.

He told her that her imagination that she had used a thousand of times, the same imagination that had the ability to take her anywhere was the secret ingredient belonging to the mind. How she had already encountered the emotional matrix, the place where he had seen her visit many times, from sliding down kitchen walls, to giving a shit. It was the place where he had watched her endlessly trying to unravel the emotional vines and trying to figure it out. He told her that the emotional matrix was the secret ingredient belonging to the body. Then he stopped.

There was silence. She could not understand why he had stopped so she asked him why. The silence broke and his response was simple. He told her he was conferring with the mind, because thinking just with the heart is lazy and the very reason why many souls find themselves in hot water. "This is something we would like to change". In your case we are going to move forward, because in the end having the ability to communicate effectively with the mind regarding matters of the heart, means the emotional matrix for you will become less complicated" he said. She laughed and thought that the whole experience was extraordinary. She had seen many people, especially women think with their hearts and those who did often ended up emotionally fucked up trying to unravel it all and spent a tremendous amount of time searching for a way out of the emotional matrix.

She waited a few seconds for this extraordinary conferring process to finish. She had no idea what 'The Heart' and mind were conferring and she did not care because she was not that curious, now wondered if taming her curiosity was such a good thing. Suddenly she heard words of conviction 'The Heart' "The heart is the secret ingredient belonging to every soul," he said.

He told her that when one has the ability to connect the secret ingredients belonging to the mind, body and soul only then do they have the ability so seek a True Sense of self. For her, it was inspiration that had created the connection, but for others it may be something totally different. Some never make the connection at all is where he ended.

She had so many other questions but the main question at the forefront of her mind was the purpose of the secret ingredients belonging to the mind, body and soul. So he wrote it down;

The imagination has the ability to take you anywhere: It can take you places that are limitless. It can show you numbers. It can foresee outcomes. It can give you pictures. It can change your pathways. It can unlock your dreams. It can make you question. It allows you to hear unspoken voices. It can make you see the unseen. It can tap into the emotional matrix. It is governed by the heart. (Without the heart it would not function)

The emotional matrix only shows you your true emotions. It can steer your choices. It can trigger responses (anger, crying, revenge, compassion and so on) It can make you confused. It can make you Love. It can create barriers. It can make you hate. It can cause conflict with the mind. It can keep you a prisoner. It can create obsessions. It can show your fears. It allows you to hear (the words of others) and it can poison your soul. It too is governed by the heart.

The Heart is the genius that guides you to the mysteries you cannot see. It can help you build relationships that exist within. It can alert you when your soul cries. It can tell you right from wrong. It has a close relationship with the emotional matrix. It is the only link to intuition.

It can open up your internal world. It is the ruler of all existence. It tells you what your eyes see. It communicates with all three celestial bodies (the mind, body and soul) and it tells you whether you live or die:

It lives in every soul. It chooses when it stops beating. It pumps Love juice around the body's solar system and when used incorrectly it can poison your soul. It is the Heart that is at the centre of everything and when a connection has been made, bringing the mind, Body and soul and their secret ingredients together, it creates an alignment which allows you to explore who you truly are.

He added; you need the imagination to take you there and you need to use your emotional matrix to unravel the emotional vines correctly to feel the truth. You need to follow your heart to explore the mysteries that one cannot see. They all work together and bounce around. Although they do not work in an orderly manner usually, when a connection has been made, they do, and this is the reason you are exposed to mysteries about the legends and stories that are linked to your soul and it is these that truly define you is where the list ended.

She was amazed and in awe of the whole experience but it was now her Curiosity that was at the forefront of her mind, generating one question to put to 'The Heart of the Tiger'. "If you are the Heart, why do you call yourself the Heart of the Tiger'?

Answer; you were born in the month of October, the Chinese month of the Tiger. It is one legend amongst many that belongs to you.

CHAPTER 26

Making the Connection (Pathway of Alignment)

Standing on the pathway of alignment, holding the hand belonging to 'The Heart of the Tiger' with one hand and holding the list in the other, they were waiting. She did not know exactly what they were waiting for, but they were waiting. Her environment was strange the pathway on which they stood led to nowhere because a couple of inches from their feet there was nothing.

She defined it as nothing because there was nothing; just cold air that rose from beneath her feet and brushed upwards from her feet to her head, touching both sides of her face as it passed. Her environment was colourless. It wasn't white nor was it grey. There was nothing but her, 'The Heart of the Tiger' and this air for company.

She became very emotional she was not sure why, except the environment where she was now standing saddened her. She sensed that this kind of environment had been created prior to her standing at the very beginning of the pathway of alignment. She knew she had not created it because she recognised that she was creative, from painting pictures over the horizon, to creating patterns on her jeans. She sensed this environment had been created by something that had the ability to erase things. She could not put her finger on it. She sensed that whatever had been there before had been erased in phases over a long period of time.

Suddenly she felt a vibration beneath her feet. The cold air changed to warm and there was a loud rumbling noise. Before her very eyes she witnessed the connection wall approaching from the gap where the pathway of alignment ended and she knew it was the connection wall because she had a good sense of ownership. This belonged to her.

The connection wall positioned itself at the end of the pathway. Standing tall, she could see how the connections were made. Three horizontal lines were marked on the connection wall, showing sections that belonged to the mind, body and soul. She could not tell which section of the wall belonged to which as they were not labelled. The connection wall blocked the pathway and she thought that her curiosity had led her to another dead end.

Suddenly the connection wall started to move, the top section folded into the second section and the second folded itself into the first like a transformer. The connection wall had transformed itself into a small block at the end of the pathway. She questioned if she was meant to jump over it because she could not see any other logical explanation as to why it would do that. It did not make sense to jump over it; there was nothing on the other side. Then she heard music. She had no idea where it was coming from but she knew what she had heard. It was soulful music. The music triggered the most extraordinary thing.

The environment that she believed to give her a sense of sadness was changing.

The not so white and not so grey was pealing from the atmosphere and as it pealed in front of her eyes, to her amazement, she saw bright, vibrant colours that had been hidden. Colourless was falling and in its place colourful appeared around her. She cried. She cried because she knew exactly what those colours represented. They were her true colours and even though she was not sure as to what these colours meant or the stories they told, she knew that they were hers.

During this experience 'The Heart of the Tiger' confirmed that they were her true colours that had been erased over a long period of time. It had all started from when she had left her last peak experience and had continued whilst she was searching for her respectful place in the world. He also said that the pathways she had walked had led her here and her ability to question everything had exposed her to the mysteries of life and brought her closer to finding her True Definition.

In awe of her true colours, what now caught her attention was a small connection wall that was at the end of the pathway, a few feet from where they stood. Now wondering about its purpose, it started to move. She could not work out what the connection wall was doing (maybe it too had lost its true sense of identity) and she found herself trying to understand its logic. Trying to understand someone else's logic is what she had done for most her life, especially in relation to men and their behaviour. It was only when she started to question something's logic did she dabble. (Outside the box)

Suddenly there was a bright light coming from the small connection wall. Within seconds of her seeing this bright light, the connection wall had re shaped itself. In her amazement the connection wall had completed the pathway of alignment and connected itself to what she defined as the pathway to nowhere. She knew this was it. She was going to find out who she truly was and it was her imagination that had brought her here. Holding onto the hand that belonged to 'The Heart of the Tiger' she walked the pathway of alignment belonging to the mind, body and soul.

CHAPTER 27

A True Definition (Her internal Caves)

Walking within the atmosphere that projected her true colours and following the pathway belonging to the mind, body and soul, she defined it as a real soul searching experience. She was searching for the answers and she knew they existed within her atmosphere. After all, she was walking amongst her true colours.

She did not know how the truth was going to show itself but she did notice that her intuition was strong and that she trusted it completely. Intuition had been something she had experience many times. It had been strong in some cases and not so strong in others. Previously she had always had an issue with her intuition because it was the one thing she had always doubted. She fought with herself many times and often found herself in a tizwoz; all tangled up, knowing one day and not knowing the next day. She believed that on many occasions her intuition had left her feeling confused, to the point where she had to question it. She questioned it because she doubted herself and her ability to be on point when it came to her intuition. In the past this had everything to do with other people's abilities to doubt her judgements. Men doubted her judgement when she insisted that he was cheating. Her parents doubted her judgement in relation to everything. Friends doubted her judgements with regards to other friends and some employers doubted her with regards to her ideas. All these previous experiences had contributed to her doubting her intuition.

(Walking the pathway of alignment, she knew she should have never questioned her institution because regardless of how strong or not so strong it was, it had very rarely been wrong)

Grasping that it was ok to trust her intuition, she had to believe that her intuition was right, that this was her mission and the pathway that followed on from this experience led to her destiny. She was destined to do something. It was going to be something legendary and bigger than just finding out who she truly was. She had led herself to believe that finding the True Sense of Self was her only mission because she wanted to show something to the world. It was, but now having total confidence in her intuition, she knew there was something bigger in store for her.

Trying to embrace the experience and walking the pathway of alignment, her intuition sensed something was going to happen. Suddenly a door appeared to her right and she smiled because it was a sign that her intuition had been right. The door to the right had just appeared from nowhere. It was made from pure crystals which were small and tiny and glistened as she looked at them. They reminded her of the place she used to go called 'The Magic land of Alice'. For a brief moment she reflected on those times. Her autographical memory linked to her episodic memory and for a few seconds she was travelling down pathway's to the place that was limitless.

Once she had stopped reflecting, she pushed the silver button that was labelled Internal Cave One. The button had been brought to her attention by her intuition but it was her curiosity who was telling her to press it, whilst getting out his guns, not knowing what stood before them. The door slid open and she waited. Again her curiosity became too much and she walked in.

The Cave of Saturn:

She stood behind the door holding the hand of 'The Heart of the Tiger. She had no idea what this place was or how it related to her. She could vaguely see images in the distance but she could not make them out because there was not a lot of light. Internal Cave One was dim and this made her feel uncomfortable.

Suddenly the light became brighter for a few seconds. But the light went away as quickly as it had appeared. This changing of the light caused Internal Cave One to glow a warm golden colour. The few seconds of brightness repeated itself very much like the light belonging to that of a lighthouse. When it was bright for a few seconds, it was bright enough for her to see the path that existed beneath her feet.

The path on which she stood was shiny, gold and strange. She bent down to feel it with her fingers and to her amazement the path on which she stood was made from satin. She took off her shoes and rubbed her feet on the ground, twisting them as if to indulge herself in pure luxury. She could not help but smile and with a simple "Mmmm" she believed that wherever she was, it was a good start.

When she had finished indulging her feet, it was 'The Heart of the Tiger' who explained where she was. He told her that Internal Cave

One gave her the ability to communicate to the universe every time she felt lost or when things did not make sense. He told her Internal Cave One was the telephone line that linked to planet Saturn, the true home belonging to her soul that existed in the universe. (According to 'The Heart of the Tiger' this was the place she had been before she had started her journey in the real world)

The Cave of Saturn was home to thousands of beautiful women with diverse personalities who are individually different but all accustomed to the planets way of life. Saturn was a place where everything is pure and a place where there are no boundaries. Planet Saturn has no rules, expectations or limitations. Women are free to express themselves and nothing is deemed strange or out of the ordinary.

Women from Saturn are exposed to riches that belong to the planet. No one is excluded from learning the true meaning of something. Oppression and limitations are forbidden. Many are taught the true meaning of love, friendship, right and wrong, good and bad and the meaning of being true to themselves, regardless of how strange they may be deemed by those who are not from Saturn. These are the ways of the women who come from this planet. This is a life that they have been accustomed to, a life that has shaped their personalities and beliefs.

(When women feel lost or confused, many question themselves. They often tear themselves down and are still none the wiser as to why shit happens. They relive the event or situation in their head, checking and double checking themselves and then blame themselves. Often sending them into the Cave of Darkness or to the place of 'nothing I do is good enough'. But for those who embark on the pathway of deeper questioning, they turn to the universe. With the knowledge that everything happens for a reason)

Internal Cave One was the true link between herself and those who she believed were watching over her. This had everything to do with the fact that she was one of the thousands of women whose soul came from Saturn. 'The Heart of the Tiger' confirmed that planet Saturn is where her guides were waiting to provide her with signs, should she ask. Signs that would help her to gain a better understanding, identify life lessons, give the gift of a miracle or provide an answer to things that did not make sense.

Not all women are the same and it is general knowledge. This is because some women come from the planet Venus. They have a different type of beauty, personality and way of life. They are very different in their ways and have not been exposed to the same things as those women from Saturn. They have been exposed to some limitations and they have been taught different things but even so, they share the same desires to those women who are from Saturn. These desires include the desire of love, friendship and a true sense of self. The only difference between these women is that those from Venus are confused as to what it looks like.

She shamefully admitted that all men are from mars and this is why the legendary John Grey (Women are from Venus and Men are from Mars) is able to explain the psychological differences between men and women. However he did not explore the women who are from Saturn, which is why his book was questionable in her opinion.

Now, she knew why she felt different to some women. She didn't think like them, act like them, behave like them, respond like them, look like them, share the same beliefs as them and in many cases, she didn't put up with the same shit as them. Having explored Internal Cave One she concluded that the women, to whom she believed she was different, were from Venus.

Having heard the mysteries of Internal Cave One and having a better understanding of how the Cave of Saturn related to her, her emotional matrix was calm and peaceful. She did not yet know how she truly felt about coming from Saturn but she was grateful for what she had learned about herself. She had gained a better understanding of why she had felt alienated from certain types of women and why when she felt lost she often found herself talking to the universe.

Exploring her first internal cave had created a hunger to explore others. Thanks to her curiosity she demanded that 'The Heart of the Tiger show her what this cave looked like, as she could not see it properly in the dim light. He obliged, and Internal Cave One lit up. The path on which she stood was floating amongst the images she could not see before. Images that had been black and white were now images of colour. Colourful planets were showing themselves to her in their true form, spinning slowly in the atmosphere, accompanied by a thousand stars. This was the universe according to the world of definition.

Before she had time to take in the view of Internal Cave One or embrace planet Saturn she saw a door appear to her right as it had done so before. This door looked like a clone of the last. The only difference was that the silver button on the door read Internal Cave Two.

She checked with her intuition and asked if she should continue what she defined as her soul searching experience. She was encouraged to follow through. She noticed that the caves were numbered but she had no idea where these caves led, causing her to become anxious. She remembered that 'The Heart of the Tiger' had previously told her that not all caves were pleasant and it was this thought that left her standing in Internal Cave One, contemplating.

She felt her emotional matrix change from calm to unsure and her emotional vines moving like they had been awakened by her uncertainty. For the first time in a long time her unflattering forehead appeared. She had no idea what was waiting for her in Internal Cave Two and her imagination could not provide her with a playful training ground. This was her truth and she knew deep down the truth could not be manipulated during the soul searching experience.

Although her imagination could not foresee what was in Internal Cave Two, her imagination reminded her why she was doing it. It provided short image formations to encourage her to move on. She saw the tags of ownership on those who were lost and those acting like clones. She saw those striving to earn a respectful place in the world, those who had something to prove and those who were willing to start somewhere. She saw those who had visited 'nothing I do is good enough' and those who were asking why they did it. She saw those who were searching for the truth and those asking where internal happiness lived.

The image formations ended and her emotional matrix was wide awake. They had stirred many emotions within her and regardless of how anxious she had been, she proceeded to Internal Cave Two

The Cave of Sexuality

She found herself standing in water that run like a river through the heart of the cave in which she stood. The water was a turquoise blue and rippled against her body as if it were dancing with her knees. She watched it for a few seconds, trying to shift her state of mind from the place where she had just come from to the place where she was now standing. She thought about how extraordinary it was that as one door closes, another one opens. She wondered how it was possible that the opening and closing of doors had the power to guide you to the place you were meant to be.

Internal Cave Two signified that she was now embarking on the pathway of deeper questioning whilst standing in the water. She felt that the opening and closing of doors took you to the place you needed to be to experience new things and was geared to show and teach you something. The place you needed to be that would question everything. This thought led her to question the order in which her internal caves were being shown. Why had it been Internal Cave One that she had explored first and why was she now standing in water?

Standing in water, she saw lights flickering in between the rocks. The flickering lights were candles that she deemed to be dancing an African dance. The flames' heads moved from side to side and back and forth as if they were dancing in her honour. Her emotional matrix was stirring. She was not quite sure what was happening in the matrix but she had felt this feeling before. With water up to her knees she felt aroused and was conscious that she was biting her bottom lip and felt rather horny. She had the desire to touch herself but aware that she was in the company of three characters belonging to her (The Heart of the Tiger, her Intuition and her Curiosity) she bent down into the water and gently splashed her face and arms.

She laughed to herself because she knew that this type of intervention had never worked in the past. She had tried it many times before. Trying to resist what she was now defining as sexual tension (because the biting of the bottom lip and her overwhelming desire to touch her breast with one hand and masturbate with the other was a sign that a form of sexual tension was present in this cave), her imagination began wondering down the tunnel that led to her deepest sexual fantasies. She had no idea where this cave was going to lead or why she was here, but she did know that this cave was linked to her sexually somehow.

As her imagination disappeared down tunnels and her sexual desires became more extreme, she was hoping that at the end of this internal cave she would be given the opportunity to release these desires. The thought of having to mediate a fight between sexual tension and the libido gave her a headache. (Headache the most common excuse for women with low libidos' and those suffering from sexual tension)

Desperate to explore Internal Cave Two as quickly as possible, she walked through the blue water whilst looking at the candles that were still dancing. She embraced the water and dragged her finger tips though the ripples of water as she walked. The further she walked the more sexual her behaviour became. She caressed the cave wall with her fingers all the while breathing deeply, causing her body to receive unexplainable sexual sensations. She began to feel delusional and felt that this cave had the potential to give her the best sexual experience ever (in the way of MIND SEX).

Mind sex; the new craze she had heard about where hundreds of women were unlocking their mind to trigger orgasms all over the place. The internet had hidden secrets that only those who had embarked on the pathway to deeper questioning would find. Women who got sick of men asking for directions could identify numerous ways to have an orgasm because mind sex empowered these women to meet their own sexual desires. Mind sex was the best kept secret to great sex and the secret ingredient to unlimited orgasms.

Contemplating mind sex, she continued to walk through Internal Cave Two. She did not need to ask 'The Heart of the Tiger' where she was because she knew exactly where she was for she had all the symptoms of someone who was horny and sexuality frustrated.

Suddenly she noticed that the colour of the water was changing and it was this that had her questioning where she was. Blue was now turning into pink so she walked faster questioning the cave and herself. The soul searching experience was far more complex than she had expected. She had believed the caves would state the obvious but the things that were happening during the cave experience had left her questioning. She knew that she could execute the experience at any time. She had expected the caves to make her want to turn away because the truth was too painful. Despite this, she decided that she was not there yet and must go on.

(She believed that growing up in the smudge had trained her to believe that when shit hurts, really hurts then you are dealing with the truth. It is only when you have reached the point, where the truth is too painful, do you make a conscious decision to face it or run from it).

Surrounded by pink water, her curiosity caused her to turn round and try and work out where the transition had taken place. The blue water travelled from behind her into the distance. It was very strange but she carried on walking. She mentally compared the pink water to the blue and how the blue water had been cold and rough; giving her the impression the ripples of water had tried to work against her. Flowing in the opposite direction and making it hard for her to balance. On the other hand, the pink water was warmer, calmer and more willing to work in harmony with her movements, not to mention it was slightly prettier.

During the comparing process she sensed that she was nearing the end of the cave and was somewhat pissed off. She believed that she had learnt nothing other than the differences in water colour and behaviour patterns. Maybe she had missed something. It was possible that she had not paid attention to detail, given that her imagination had been travelling down tunnels most of the time, having another form of mind sex. So if she had learnt nothing, what had been the point?

Suddenly, she saw something moving in the water ten foot from where she stood. Her thought process was now doing the think and skip from mermaids to sea demons. What the hell was that? She wished that she could take back her words in saying that this cave had taught her nothing. She sensed that whatever it was, it was going to be the very thing that was sent to teach her something. She watched as the figure drew closer to where she was standing. She didn't dare to move and tried to calm herself because she knew that panicking would only blur her mind into disorder (something she had learnt whilst developing her book of predators).

She saw the stay calm pages appear one after another and she knew that her action pages had been written as a result of a calm moment. Therefore, she knew that staying calm enabled her to think clearly about the action needed should she need to get herself out of this situation or kick the shit out of something to save her life.

Whilst flicking through her book of predators, she breathed slowly and deeply, picking out the action pages should this unknown figure be dangerous. The figure drew nearer still, keeping beneath the water as if to not yet to expose itself. Using her scanning techniques, she homed in on the unidentified figure and tried to work out its movements. The more she looked, the more confused she became. She tried to link the figure to her environment but she still had no idea as to what it was. It was then that she recognised the figure of a female and before she could go on questioning, the unknown figure had risen from beneath the water bed and presented itself in her moment.

As the naked figure of the woman emerged from the water, she admired the beauty of the person who was now standing in front of her. She was in awe of this person's presence and the unknown figure opened her arms as if to welcome her. As the unknown figure stretched out her arms, a magnetic force sent vibrations all through her body. It was the first time ever that she believed that someone had the ability to touch all her senses (mentally, spiritually and emotionally). These vibrations also tapped into her libido causing it to be at its highest ever and with no words needed, they both took part in what was probably one of the best lesbian experiences ever.

They kissed each other with a passion and pulled each other's hair in sexual aggression. Her tongue wondered from the mouth to the neck and followed the outline of the body until it reached a place that was tasteful. Even though she found it hard to breathe, she had this overwhelming willingness to please and as much as her tongue was sore, the unknown figure wanted more.

The breast was now a place to embrace femininity and she rose from between the mountains and gave a kiss of affection. If she had been a man, this new power of seduction would have most definitely created an erection. As they intertwined and embraced their femininity, it did not seem strange or out of the ordinary. Their emotional matrixes were exploding and touch was like a form of decoding that opened doors to sexual places, that she could not recall having ever been explored before.

The feelings she experienced in this moment were everything she had dreamt of. Being touched in a way that sent shivers down her spine, the feeling of being understood, not on one level but all levels enthralled her. This experience had brought her what women wanted and what every woman was searching for; Trust. It was not just about sex. There was no desire to fast forward to what would happen next or have "how will I feel when they leave my bed?" She knew there would be no feeling of neglect flowed by "when will I see you next?"

She believed that no matter what man she had been with, there had always been something missing. The men she had encountered had the tendency to make women feel like they were being used. She believed that this was a wiring fault in most men and thanks to the wiring of men; she had often questioned what it would be like to meet a man who was in touch with his feminine side. (No longer having to question, if the wires belonging to men were actually connected to everything)

She blamed the world of definition for setting up women to fail in the cave of love and sexuality. Programming the mind into believing that only men can be with women to achieve a 'happy ever after' and this was wrong in her opinion.

So many things in her life had projected that only men had the ability to meet the needs of women. In the real world, sex is the primary connection between most men and women because sex does not question the differences in psychological development. However for most women, sex is not enough and with most men failing to meet the psychological and emotional needs of women, this is the very reason why most women feel unloved, misunderstood and questioning why they even put up with their shit.

Her sexual encounter with the unknown female had ended and it ended just as she wanted it to. The experience had showed her what it was like to connect with someone on all levels. There was no need to give directions, communicate her feelings or question anything. Her soul had been free to experience something rare and extraordinary that she had always wanted to experience in the place called love. Despite this feeling, Internal Cave Two had left her slightly confused because she had never previously been sexually attracted to women.

She sat on a rock, blaming Internal Cave Two for fucking with her head and added DIKE to all the other definitions she had collected. She could almost feel the word DIKE on her forehead and she contemplated the reaction of those close to her should the word DIKE escape from

Internal Cave Two. She tried to think up every other word that could be an alternative to the one she had given herself. She concluded that she would find a much prettier word than DIKE, should it escape and she would manipulate the word to one that had no definition, believing where there is no definition, there is no box and therefore there is no label.

This particular Internal Cave had affected her mood and it was evident that she was becoming aware that the soul searching experience can either make you or break you. 'The Heart of the Tiger' appeared to explain things to her. "Internal Cave Two was to teach you about fluid sexuality" he said. She sat on the rock and listened. "Fluid sexuality does not mean you are confused, gay, bisexual or bi-curious". (Random words 'The Heart of the Tiger' stated were created by man just to titillate his imagination). "Fluid Sexuality means that your sexuality can change". "You could be sexually attracted to men for years, months or even days but somewhere you find yourself being attracted to women or vice versa".

"There are no timescales relating to fluid sexuality; it could last a month or even years until it reverts back to the way it was before it changed." He explained that she was one of thousands of woman who had a fluid sexuality, hence why there was a high increase of women leaving their husbands and boyfriends to have relationships with women. He told her not to be surprised and that one day she may find herself embracing long term relationships with women, if not many one night stands. She laughed and told him not to be silly. Her alter ego had raised its ugly head and was trying to convince 'The Heart of the Tiger' that she was not Gay, confused, Bi-sexual or bi- curious.

She did not quite buy into the idea of women and men having this thing called fluid sexuality and she said so. 'The Heart of the Tiger's' response was simple, "That was not water that led you through Internal Cave Two, that was love juice". Love juice was a term used by those in the Smudge.

Love juice had to be taken seriously. If someone mentioned love juices then the feelings were real. She hated the fact that 'The Heart of the Tiger' had the ability to use terms that he knew would hit home and regardless of how Internal Cave Two had affected her and questioned everything. She knew whether she liked it or not, her soul searching experience was based on the truth.

As before, a door appeared on the right and it indicated that it was time to move on.

CHAPTER 28

The Ultimate Definition of Self (Her internal Caves)

Stepping through the door of Internal Cave Three, she could hear the laughter of children and although she could not see them, she could hear them. She heard names being called but for some reason it was the same name and she had not realised that it was the same name being called until she actually took the time to listen.

Voices, somewhere in the distance seemed to be looking for the same person. The voices echoed and bounced off the rainbow which created a bridge in the distance. Suddenly she caught a glimpse of a little girl who was sitting on the grass to the right of her. She questioned if this was the person that everyone was looking for. Surely the little girl could hear them calling her name, assuming this was the little girl the voices were calling out for.

Questioning who this little girl was and wanting to know where she was, she thought the little girl would have the answers. She believed having the answers meant she could move through the cave quicker and wouldn't have to work everything out for herself. This was because deep down she wanted to end the soul searching experience and that had everything to do with Internal Cave Two, but felt she couldn't (not until she had found the caves that scared the shit out of her) The caves that 'The Heart of the Tiger' had mentioned earlier.

Ending the soul searching experience had more to do with being scared that if she learnt the truth about who she really was, she may not like who she was. Regardless, it was better than living with others definition of who she was. She knew that as she travelled, the caves were destined to become more challenging and leaving the soul searching experience was not an option at this point (well not until she had found the caves that scared the shit out of her). Only then would she believe she would have done enough to escape the feeling of failure.

Now in the little girl's moment, she sat down beside her and said nothing. She was surprised to find the little girl did not acknowledge her presence. She waited, whilst questioning if the little girl had a hearing problem, or a personality that was deemed rude and arrogant. "How old are you," she asked. "Seven," the little girl responded. Trying to engage in a conversation with this seven year old girl she had never met was difficult. The little girl only gave answers when asked and all the while her tone of voice was somewhat irritating.

She thought it was funny that the little girl had dark spiral hair and green eyes, just as she did when she was about her age and tried to use this as a starting point to get the answers she was looking for. When she asked why the little girl was sitting there, the little girl claimed to be waiting and when asked what she was waiting for, the little girl replied she was waiting for the seven year cycle.

Before she had time to process that statement in her head, the little girl held out her arms and cupped her hands together. She watched a fireball of light present itself in the palms belonging to the little girl. Having defined the little girl as rude, arrogant and now unpredictable, she questioned if she should get up and run. All the while the little girl watched the fireball of light and then closed her palms together as quick as she had opened them. She asked the little girl about the fireball of light she cradled in the palm of her hands, curious to know and better, understand where she was.

Failing to get an answer it was "What is the seven year cycle?" that flowed from her lips. The little girl stood up. "You'll see," she said whilst flicking her curls and cutting her eye and with that the little girl ran off into the distance. She had not got the answers she needed to move through Internal Cave Three quickly and was none the wiser as to where she was. She didn't even manage to get the little girl's name. She wished she had asked the right questions because she was sensing that the name of the seven year old girl that was important and held the secret to why she was there.

Heading towards the rainbow, the only landmark she could see that had any significance, she passed another girl who was dancing by a tree. This young girl was older than the last and she was laughing and twirling, all the while smiling and projecting that she had a lot of energy and some form of internal happiness. Approaching the young girl, desperately looking for answers, (the answers she had failed to obtain from the seven year old girl she had met previously) she was greeted by a warm angelic smile.

She thought this girl's behaviour was typical of a young girl who had not yet embarked on a journey in the real world. The real world would be sure to slap the smile off her face. Therefore this young girl's behaviour to her was deemed strange, little did she know that she too had once projected this same behaviour but she had simply forgotten. Before she had a chance to introduce herself or ask the young girl any questions, the young girl told her she was waiting. Not only did she tell her she was waiting, she told her age, where she lived, people she liked and she talked about the rainbow and its purpose.

This was a fourteen year old girl who was excited about life and everyday was a great day. There was always something to explore and learn about in the world she lived in and this was a young girl who believed the world was magical. She asked the young girl if she could help her. The young girl claimed that she would do anything she could to help, but it would have to wait until she had received. The more she looked at this young girl, who she was now defining as a typical teenager, the more she became curious.

She was curious because she believed she had seen this young girl somewhere else and thinking hard and opening her mind, the young girl looked very much like the seven year old girl she had met previously. "What is your name?" she asked. The question was lost in translation because whilst she was thinking hard and opening her mind, the young girl was now looking into the palm of her hands and again she witnessed the same event that had taken place previously.

Stir crazy and not having a clue what was going on she waited for the young girl to close the palms of her hands, so she could ask the young girl questions that provoked answers. She was told that the fireball of light happened every seven years and was known as the seven year cycle which was paramount to personal growth. The young girl claimed that it was important to embrace it, hence why she had been waiting for it. Now she had received it, she could continue her journey to the next stage and then in seven years' time, the same process would happen again.

Finding this information hard to grasp because this fourteen year old girl had the tendency to speed things up and miss things out, like someone with high energy levels that seemed to be fuelled by passion. She could not make the connection between the information she had been given, Internal Cave Three and herself. The young girl claimed she had to be somewhere and she was sorry she couldn't keep her promise to help her. Upon saying these words the fourteen year old girl disappeared through a hole in the tree. She deemed Internal Cave Three as weird; she had met two girls who were seven years apart in age and both had shared the same event (creating fireballs in the palm of their hands). What is this place and how does it relate to me? She questioned.

Somewhat pissed off ,with her mind doing the think and skip trying to make the connection, she continued to venture Internal Cave Three and headed towards the rainbow. She walked on for a while and had not seen anyone else. She still heard the voices; however there was something different the sound of children's laughter. It had become faint and the further she walked, the fainter they became. She noticed that all she could really hear were the voices of those who were calling the name of someone who had obviously not been found yet. She didn't get it. Nonetheless, she headed to the rainbow and just maybe, things would make sense.

She passed three other girls along the way and all were seven years older than the last. It was obvious what they were doing and she did not feel the need to stop because she knew that they were waiting, waiting for the seven year cycle. She was on the verge of giving up. She looked up hoping to see the rainbow and she could not believe what she saw. The rainbow was now behind her and she did not recall walking under it. She believed that this internal cave could be the one that broke her. She was tired and had enough. She knew she could leave the experience anytime she wanted, but she knew that should she leave, she would have failed.

Accepting that somehow the rainbow had shifted from in front to behind, she sat down and thought. She took time to reflect on that she had seen, hoping to come up with the answer as to where she was and how Internal Cave Three related to her. Image formations were forming, opening her autobiographic and episodic memory, where she spent some time piecing things together.

Suddenly it all made sense and she knew where she was. This was going to be the first time during the whole soul searching experience that she had learnt to recognise signs and make the connections. More importantly it was going to be the first time that she would experience how powerful it is when you have the ability to access areas of the autobiographical and episodic memory that have never been used. It all made sense. She was in The Cave of Name.

The first young girl she had met was her when she was seven; rude and arrogant is what she was. The fireball of light was her first encounter involving the seven year cycle, where the fireball that projected itself in the palm of her hands told a story which taught her about the seven year cycle and informed her that it happened every seven years and she must be there to embrace it.

The second girl she had met was her at the age of fourteen, excited about life and curious. The hole in the tree had led to 'The Magic land of Alice', the place that led to secret passage ways and was limitless. However, after the age of seven the fireball of light did not tell stories, instead it gave you a seven year destiny and was related to the name you had been given at birth. (Unforeseen pathways in the palm of your hands were created just for you) in order for you to experience what you were meant to.

The pathways were calculated and shaped by using your birth name as it was the secret ingredient to form your life journey. Therefore there are no mistakes. Everything is as it should be and every seven years provoke new pathways relating to personal growth, where lessons are there to be learnt and experiences are created to teach you something, all in aid of helping you to reach your seven year destiny.

(This is why young girls from the age of fourteen were waiting, excited and curious to embark on a journey, where they hoped their dreams would guide them to what they believed to be their destiny and a place of internal happiness)

She had always believed that there was only ever one destiny, but Internal Cave Three had challenged this idea. She now believed that everyone's destiny changed every seven years in line with the seven year cycle, relating to personal growth. She also had learnt from exploring Internal Cave Three that not all pathways led to internal happiness. This had everything to do with the last three girls she had passed who were all waiting. She sensed that their waiting was more to do with hoping that the next seven year cycle was going to be better than the last, concluding that not all destinies are destined to be great. However, where you ended up, was a sign that you are where you were meant to be, holding the lessons you had to learn that related to your personal growth.

Her emotional matrix vibrated strongly because for the first time during her soul searching experience, she had learned to use the lessons and now she believed this was how she was to become a master of herself. As for the name that she heard being called, it was the name her grandmother had given her, Cherry. She had just simply forgotten. As for the children's laughter fading into the distance, it was a symbol that she forgotten how much she used to laugh.

Doors appeared, caves were explored and each time she was learning how to master them. In mastering the internal caves, she was in turn learning to become a master of herself.

Her ability to see the signs, make the connections, embrace the good and the bad and each time learn who she really was, changed the colour of her soul.

The doubting of herself disappeared, the labels she had not even written crumbled, the something to prove was locked up in an institution, the painful shit was sent into oblivion, the place of 'nothing I do is good enough' was condemned and knocked down and the feeling of failure was no longer present. The list went on. More importantly she learnt how to make choices based on a True Definition and not the world's definition of her.

CHAPTER 29

A Taste of freedom

Having freed herself from her soul searching experience, she was waiting. She was waiting for Tasha and Joanne to arrive because Tanya was being released from prison. As she waited, she flicked through the photo book she kept in her head to admire the image formations of how she had found a True sense of self.

For the last time she used her ABCs to recall how she had found a True Sense of self. She had mastered her ABCs and that led to giving Tasha the ABC formula. It was for wanting to become a master of self that had increased the power of her imagination that created the playground of "I wonder If"". It was the inspiration in Tanya's letter that had created the pathway of alignment, where she encountered the secret ingredients that led to the internal caves. Her sheer determination and willingness to explore the internal caves led to the secret ingredients that truly define her and is where she had found the formula in finding a True Sense of Self.

This was her moment. She smiled. At the age of thirty five, the soul searching experience, had not only given her the formula of how to find a True Definition it had also reminded her that she was to embrace a forthcoming seven year cycle where unknown pathways would form and she would embark on a new journey. She Hoped, this seven year cycle would be better than the last.

Arriving at the prison gates with Tasha and Joanne for company, four women who had all grown up in the smudge were going to be together again for the first time in years. Joanne was already laughing and making predictions of how Tanya would make a grand exit. They all agreed that if prison had changed Tanya somehow, the patois that flowed from a white girl lips would help to identify her.

Tasha explained that she was going to use the ABC formula as an excuse for the lack of letters she had written to Tanya and how she had been so busy trying to master it; she has lost herself in the process. This excuse was deemed hilarious. Tasha went on to explain that although the ABC formula had helped to foresee the pathway to having another baby and was the reason why she had chosen to have a termination, she had also been busy using the ABC formula to foresee other pathways relating to a number of men. As a result her choice in men was getting better.

She knew that Tasha was never going to change when it came to men. Tasha had an addiction and she believed strongly that until Tasha reached a point in her life where the ABC formula was not enough, only then would Tasha ask if anyone knew the 'True Sense of Self'.

The noise of the prison gates rumbled. It was general knowledge that anything involved with the prison system took a long time and that included releasing prisoners. Whilst they were waiting, her imagination was disappearing down new tunnels and her dysfunctional relationship with her curiosity was once again eager to start a new journey that involved the forthcoming seven year cycle. She did not know when she would encounter this cycle but she knew it was coming. She could feel it and she knew it was coming to teach her something.

The shouts that she recognised as a form of communication between women from the smudge steered her away from her curiosity, the seven year cycle and the unknown pathways to her seven year destiny. Approaching from the prison gate was Tanya who was smiling timidly, as if she was trying to mask the shame of only having two plastic bags to show for her time in prison.

All three of the girls knew the rules of the smudge when it came to collecting someone who was being released from prison and that was not to show too much emotion. This was for two reasons. The first had everything to do with not triggering the painful shit that was buried in the emotional matrix of most women leaving prison and the second reason was the knowledge that prison letters were used like wallpaper to brighten up the prison walls, so somewhere written on that wall was: 'you are ARD'.

It was the nudging of fists that bonded them together. Tasha claimed that the fist nudge was too painful and gave her a fag (Cigarette) instead. Even though they were now grown women, some traits of smudge behaviour were not forgotten. The nudge was a form of respect and the fag was a nice gesture. Recognition that it had been the battle of the testosterone level between the sisterhood and the brotherhood back in the 90's that had changed this particular generation of women. The days, when most young people were searching for what they believed was a true sense of identity.

Moving away from the prison gate Tanya talked about some of the funniest events that had happened whilst being in prison. Of course some of it was exaggerated because Tanya was a girl from the smudge. Tanya spoke of how the letters she had received were what kept her going. At mentioning the letters, they turned on Tasha, asking her why she had only ever sent an A4 sheet of paper about nothing. It was here Tasha used the ABC formula as an excuse and that led to a passionate cussing session.

This particular moment reminded her of their trip to Amsterdam where they had all been in a musty room, stoned enough to travel down secret passageways and re-write themselves in a parallel universe. It was this thought that had her curiosity roaming the grounds whilst her imagination ventured tunnels she believed she had not yet explored. She recognised that these were new tunnels because she was questioning if there was such a thing as a parallel universe. A parallel universe where she had heard it was possible to exist, now questioning if there was a parallel universe, were they defined differently?

This was the day they all embraced a taste of freedom. Tanya was free from prison, Joanne was free from anger, Tasha was free from choosing shit men and she was free from a world of definition.

THE SEVEN YEAR DESTINY

Arriving home it was the questioning of a parallel universe and having a sense of freedom that provoked her thoughts to revert back to the seven year cycle. Image formations started at the beginning of peak-ness, a time when she was doing whatever, where ever and to whom ever and not give a shit. Images formed themselves into a journey that told a story of how she had ended up here but more importantly how she had obtained a true sense of self.

In this moment her imagination was again making her laugh because it was here she shouted her birth name with conviction. She knew who she truly was and that her name was the secret ingredient to unforeseen pathways that led to a seven year destiny. She knew that everything was as it should be and the things that had happened previously were no mistake. She knew that no matter what she did she would always end up where she was meant to be.

At first she had not known that shouting her name with conviction in the middle of her living room would provoke the seven year destiny. But now she knew that unforeseen pathways were in the palm of her hands and she was destined to do something extraordinary.

Anything known to have the power to change the world comes from the heart and ends in "the Formula".

"A woman who conquers herself is greater than one who conquers a thousand women in battle." (Unknown)

The Formula in finding a 'True Sense of Self'

The breaking of bonds
Willingness ... Break away from what or who defines you.

The Knowing
Ability ...Know deep down you are not what they say you are.

Relationship with the enemy
Determination...Build relationships with the enemy within.

The Transition
Enthusiasm ...Unlock your mind from a world of Definition in order
to contemplate
"Change"

Recognising Change
Readiness ...Connect with your curiosity and question everything.

Knowing when to surrender
Skill ...Surrender your feelings when things don't make sense.

Recognising the Warrior
Recognise ... The warrior that exists within to explore the darkest of
caves

Make the Connection
Learn ...The lessons and embrace new things you learn about yourself.

A Taste of Freedom
Now...You have the' Formula' into finding a True Sense of Self, Con-
gratulations!

'True Sense of self',
The secret ingredient to having 'True Everything'

The Formula

"IN LOVING MEMORY"

Nicolas Venn Born Friday 13th October 1972..... Angel wings given 3rd September 2007

Genson Courtney Born 26th May 1988..... Angel wings given 4th July 2011

Robert Hilbert Born 10th August 1964.... Angel wings given 3rd may 2011

Robert Holland Born 4th February 1975..... Angel wings given 28th October 2011

THE END !

5122696R00136

Printed in Great Britain
by Amazon.co.uk, Ltd.,
Marston Gate.